THE ASCENT OF DENALI

(MOUNT McKINLEY)

Ice Fall of nearly four thousand feet, by which the upper or Harper Glacier discharges into the lower or Muldrow Glacier. (page 39)

THE ASCENT OF DENALI

(MOUNT McKINLEY)

A NARRATIVE OF THE
FIRST COMPLETE ASCENT OF THE HIGHEST
PEAK IN NORTH AMERICA

BY

HUDSON STUCK, D.D.

ARCHDEACON OF THE YUKON

ILLUSTRATED

Wolfe Publishing Co., Inc.
6471 Airpark Drive
Prescott, Arizona 86301

1988

Originally published in 1914

Wolfe Publishing Co., Inc.
Manufactured in the United States of America
ISBN: 0-935632-69-7

To

SIR MARTIN CONWAY

ONE OF THE WORLD'S GREATEST TRAVELLERS AND CLIMBERS
WHOSE FASCINATING NARRATIVES
HAVE KINDLED IN MANY BREASTS A LOVE OF THE
GREAT HEIGHTS AND A DESIRE TO ATTAIN UNTO THEM
THIS BOOK IS DEDICATED
WITH RESPECT AND ADMIRATION

PREFACE

FOREFRONT in this book, because forefront in the author's heart and desire, must stand a plea for the restoration to the greatest mountain in North America of its immemorial native name. If there be any prestige or authority in such matter from the accomplishment of a first complete ascent, "if there be any virtue, if there be any praise," the author values it chiefly as it may give weight to this plea.

It is now little more than seventeen years ago that a prospector penetrated from the south into the neighborhood of this mountain, guessed its height with remarkable accuracy at twenty thousand feet, and, ignorant of any name that it already bore, placed upon it the name of the Republican candidate for President of the United States at the approaching election—William McKinley. No voice was raised in protest, for the Alaskan Indian is inarticulate and such white men as knew the old name were absorbed in the search for gold. Some years later an officer of the United

States army, upon a reconnoissance survey into the land, passed around the companion peak, and, alike ignorant or careless of any native name, put upon it the name of an Ohio politician, at that time prominent in the councils of the nation, Joseph Foraker. So there they stand upon the maps, side by side, the two greatest peaks of the Alaskan range, "Mount McKinley" and "Mount Foraker." And there they should stand no longer, since, if there be right and reason in these matters, they should not have been placed there at all.

To the relatively large Indian population of those wide regions of the interior of Alaska from which the mountains are visible they have always borne Indian names. The natives of the middle Yukon, of the lower three hundred miles of the Tanana and its tributaries, of the upper Kuskokwim have always called these mountains "Denali" (Den-ah'li) and "Denali's Wife"—either precisely as here written, or with a dialectical difference in pronunciation so slight as to be negligible.

It is true that the little handful of natives on the Sushitna River, who never approach nearer than a hundred miles to the mountain, have another name for it. They call it *Traléika*, which, in their wholly different language, has the same signification. It is probably true of every great mountain that it bears diverse native names as one tribe or another, on this side or on that of its mighty bulk, speaks of it. But the area in which, and the people by whom, this mountain is known as Denali, preponderate so greatly as to leave no question which native name it should bear. The bold front of the mountain is so placed on the returning curve of the Alaskan range that from the interior its snows are visible far and wide, over many thousands of square miles; and the Indians of the Tanana and of the Yukon, as well as of the Kuskokwim, hunt the caribou well up on its foot-hills. Its southern slopes are stern and forbidding through depth of snow and violence of glacial stream, and are devoid of game; its slopes toward the interior of the country are mild and amene, with light snowfall and game in abundance.

Should the reader ever be privileged, as the author was a few years ago, to stand on the frozen surface of Lake Minchúmina and see these mountains revealed as the clouds of a passing snowstorm swept away, he would be overwhelmed by the majesty of the scene and at the same time deeply moved with the appropriateness of the simple native names; for simplicity is always a quality of true majesty. Perhaps nowhere else in the world is so abrupt and great an uplift from so low a base. The marshes and forests of the upper Kuskokwim, from which these mountains rise, cannot be more than one thousand five hundred feet above the sea. The rough approximation by the author's aneroid in the journey from the Tanana to the Kuskokwim would indicate a still lower level—would make this wide plain little more than one thousand feet high. And they rise sheer, the tremendous cliffs of them apparently unbroken, soaring superbly to more than twenty thousand and seventeen thousand feet respectively: Denali, "the great one," and Denali's Wife. And the little peaks in between the natives call the "children." It was on that occasion, standing spellbound at the sublimity of the scene, that the author resolved that if it were in his power he would restore these ancient mountains to the ancient people among whom they rear their heads. Savages they are, if the reader please, since "savage" means simply a forest dweller, and the author is glad himself to be a savage a great part of every year, but yet, as savages, entitled to name their own rivers, their own lakes, their own mountains. After all, these terms—"savage," "heathen," "pagan"—mean, alike, simply "country people," and point to some old-time superciliousness of the city-bred, now confined, one hopes, to such localities as Whitechapel and the Bowery.

There is, to the author's mind, a certain ruthless arrogance that grows more offensive to him as the years pass by, in the temper that comes to a "new" land and contemptuously ignores the native names of conspicuous natural objects, almost always appropriate and significant, and overlays them with names that are, commonly, neither the one nor the other. The learned societies of the world, the geographical societies, the ethnological societies, have set their faces against this practice these many years past, and to them the writer confidently appeals.

This preface must bear a grateful acknowledgment to the most distinguished of Alaskans—the man who knows more of Alaska than any other human being—Peter Trimble Rowe, seventeen years bishop of that immense territory, for the "cordial assent" which he gave to the proposed expedition and the leave of absence which rendered it possible—one more in a long list of kindnesses which have rendered happy an association of nearly ten years. Nor can better place be found for a tribute of gratitude to those who were of the little party: to Mr. Harry P. Karstens, strong, competent, and resourceful, the real leader of the expedition in the face of difficulty and danger; to Mr. Robert G. Tatum, who took his share, and more than his share, of all toil and hardship and was a most valuable colleague; to Walter Harper, Indian-bred until his sixteenth year, and up to that time trained in not much else than Henry of Navarre's training, "to shoot straight, to speak the truth; to do with little food and less sleep" (though equal to an abundance of both on occasion), who joyed in the heights as a mountain-sheep or a chamois, and whose sturdy limbs and broad shoulders were never weary or unwilling—to all of these there is heartfelt affection and deep obligation. Nor must Johnny be forgotten, the Indian boy who faithfully kept the base camp during a long vigil, and killed game to feed the dogs, and denied himself, unasked, that others might have pleasure, as the story will tell. And the name of Esaias, the Indian boy who accompanied us to the base camp, and then returned with the superfluous dogs, must be mentioned, with commendation for fidelity and thanks for service. Acknowledgment is also made to many friends and colleagues at the mission stations in the interior, who knew of the purpose and furthered it greatly and held their tongues so that no premature screaming bruit of it got into the Alaskan newspapers: to the Rev. C. E. Betticher, Jr., particularly and most warmly.

The author would add, perhaps quite unnecessarily, yet lest any should mistake, a final personal note. He is no professed explorer or climber or "scientist," but a missionary, and of these matters an amateur only. The vivid recollection of a back bent down with burdens and lungs at the limit of their function makes him hesitate to describe this enterprise as recreation. It was the most laborious undertaking with which he was ever connected; yet it was done for the pleasure of doing it, and the pleasure far outweighed the pain. But he is concerned much more with men than mountains, and would say, since "out of the fullness of the heart the mouth speaketh," that his especial and growing concern, these ten years past, is with the native people of Alaska, a gentle and kindly race, now threatened with a wanton and senseless extermination, and sadly in need of generous champions if that threat is to be averted.

CONTENTS

CHAPTER		PAGE
I.	Preparation and Approach	3
II.	The Muldrow Glacier	25
III.	The Northeast Ridge	53
IV.	The Grand Basin	80
V.	The Ultimate Height	92
VI.	The Return	117
VII.	The Height of Denali, with a Discussion of the Readings on the Summit and During the Ascent	141
VIII.	Explorations of the Denali Region and Previous Attempts at its Ascent	157
IX.	The Names Placed upon the Mountain by the Author	180

ILLUSTRATIONS

Ice fall of nearly four thousand feet by which the upper or Harper Glacier discharges into the lower or Muldrow Glacier (photogravure) . . . *Frontispiece*

FACING PAGE

The author and Mr. H. P. Karstens 4

Tatum, Esaias, Karstens, Johnny, and Walter, at the Clearwater Camp 8

Striking across from the Tanana to the Kantishna . . 12

One of the abandoned mining towns in the Kantishna 14

Denali from the McKinley fork of the Kantishna River 16

Entering the range by Cache Creek 18

The base-camp at about 4,000 feet on Cache Creek . 20

Some heads of game killed at the base-camp 22

The Muldrow Glacier. Karstens in the foreground . . 26

Ascension Day, 1913 30

Bridging a crevasse on the Muldrow Glacier 32

Hard work for dogs as well as men on the Muldrow Glacier 34

Illustrations

FACING PAGE

The Northeast Ridge shattered by the earthquake in July, 1912 40

Cutting a staircase three miles long in the ice of the shattered ridge 52

The shattered Northeast Ridge 56

Camp at 13,000 feet on Northeast Ridge 60

A dangerous passage 64

The Upper Basin reached at last. Our camp at the Parker Pass at 15,000 feet 72

Above all the range except Denali and Denali's Wife 76

Traverse under the cliffs of the Northeast Ridge to enter the Grand Basin 82

First camp in the Grand Basin—16,000 feet, looking up 84

Second camp in the Grand Basin—looking down, 16,500 feet 86

Third camp in the Grand Basin—17,000 feet, showing the shattering of the glacier walls by the earthquake . 88

The North Peak, 20,000 feet high 90

The South Peak from about 18,000 feet 94

The climbing-irons 98

Denali's Wife from the summit of Denali (photogravure) 102

Robert Tatum raising the Stars and Stripes on the highest point in North America 104

Illustrations

FACING PAGE

The saying of the Te Deum 106

Beginning the descent of the ridge; looking down 4,000 feet upon the Muldrow Glacier 122

Johnny Fred, who kept the base camp and fed the dogs and would not touch the sugar 128

"Muk," the author's pet malamute 136

Approaching the range 164

Map showing route of the Stuck-Karstens expedition to the summit of Mt. Denali (Mt. McKinley) . . . *End of volume*

THE ASCENT OF DENALI

THE ASCENT OF DENALI

CHAPTER I

PREPARATION AND APPROACH

THE enterprise which this volume describes was a cherished purpose through a number of years. In the exercise of his duties as Archdeacon of the Yukon, the author has travelled throughout the interior of Alaska, both winter and summer, almost continuously since 1904. Again and again, now from one distant elevation and now from another, the splendid vision of the greatest mountain in North America has spread before his eyes, and left him each time with a keener longing to enter its mysterious fastnesses and scale its lofty peaks. Seven years ago, writing in *The Spirit of Missions* of a view of the mountain from the Pedro Dome, in the neighborhood of Fairbanks, he said: "I would rather climb that mountain than discover the richest gold-mine in Alaska." Indeed, when first he went to Alaska it was part of the attraction which the country held for him that it contained an unclimbed mountain of the first class.

Scawfell and Skiddaw and Helvellyn had given him his first boyish interest in climbing; the Colorado and Canadian Rockies had claimed one holiday after another of maturer years, but the summit of Rainier had been the greatest height he had ever reached. When he went to Alaska he carried with him all the hypsometrical instruments that were used in the ascent as well as his personal climbing equipment. There was no definite likelihood that the opportunity would come to him of attempting the ascent, but he wished to be prepared with instruments of adequate scale in case the opportunity should come; and Hicks, of London, made them nine years ago.

Long ago, also, he had picked out Mr. Harry P. Karstens, of Fairbanks, as the one colleague with whom he would be willing to make the attempt. Mr. Karstens had gone to the Klondike in his seventeenth year, during the wild stampede to those diggings, paying the expenses of the trip by packing over the Chilkoot Pass, and had been engaged in pioneering and in travel of an arduous and adventurous kind ever since. He had mined in the Klondike and in the Seventy-Mile (hence his sobriquet of "The Seventy-Mile Kid"). It

The author and Mr. H. P. Karstens.

was he and his partner, McGonogill, who broke the first trail from Fairbanks to Valdez and for two years of difficulty and danger—dogs and men alike starving sometimes—brought the mail regularly through. When the stampede to the Kantishna took place, and the government was dilatory about instituting a mail service for the three thousand men in the camp, Karstens and his partner organized and maintained a private mail service of their own. He had freighted with dogs from the Yukon to the Iditerod, had run motor-boats on the Yukon and the Tanana. For more than a year he had been guide to Mr. Charles Sheldon, the well-known naturalist and hunter, in the region around the foot-hills of Denali. With the full vigor of maturity, with all this accumulated experience and the resourcefulness and self-reliance which such experience brings, he had yet an almost juvenile keenness for further adventure which made him admirably suited to this undertaking.

Mr. Robert G. Tatum, of Tennessee, just twenty-one years old, a postulant for holy orders, stationed at the mission at Nenana, had been employed all the winter in a determined attempt to get supplies freighted over the ice, by natives and their dog teams, to two women missionaries, a nurse and a teacher, at the Tanana Crossing. The steamboat had cached the supplies at a point about one hundred miles below the mission the previous summer, unable to proceed any farther. The upper Tanana is a dangerous and difficult river alike for navigation and for ice travel, and Tatum's efforts were made desperate by the knowledge that the women were reduced to a diet of straight rabbits without even salt. The famine relieved, he had returned to Nenana. The summer before he had worked on a survey party and had thus some knowledge of the use of instruments. By undertaking the entire cooking for the expedition he was most useful and helpful, and his consistent courtesy and considerateness made him a very pleasant comrade.

Of the half-breed boy, Walter Harper, the author's attendant and interpreter, dog driver in the winter and boat engineer in the summer for three years previous, no more need be said than that he ran Karstens close in strength, pluck, and endurance. Of the best that the mixed blood can produce, twenty-one years old and six feet tall, he took gleefully to high mountaineering, while his kindliness and invincible amiability endeared him to every member of the party.

The men were thus all volunteers, experienced

in snow and ice, though not in high-mountain work. But the nature of snow and ice is not radically changed by lifting them ten or fifteen or even twenty thousand feet up in the air.

A volunteer expedition was the only one within the resources of the writer, and even that strained them. The cost of the food supplies, the equipment, and the incidental expenses was not far short of a thousand dollars—a mere fraction of the cost of previous expeditions, it is true, but a matter of long scraping together for a missionary. Yet if there had been unlimited funds at his disposal—and the financial aspect of the affair is alluded to only that this may be said—it would have been impossible to assemble a more desirable party.

Mention of two Indian boys of fourteen or fifteen, who were of great help to us, must not be omitted. They were picked out from the elder boys of the school at Nenana, all of whom were most eager to go, and were good specimens of mission-bred native youths. "Johnny" was with the expedition from start to finish, keeping the base camp while the rest of the party was above; Esaias was with us as far as the base camp and then went back to Nenana with one of the dog teams.

The Ascent of Denali

The resolution to attempt the ascent of Denali was reached a year and a half before it was put into execution: so much time was necessary for preparation. Almost any Alaskan enterprise that calls for supplies or equipment from the outside must be entered upon at least a year in advance. The plan followed had been adopted long before as the only wise one: that the supplies to be used upon the ascent be carried by water as near to the base of the mountain as could be reached and cached there in the summer, and that the climbing party go in with the dog teams as near the 1st March as practicable. Strangely enough, of all the expeditions that have essayed this ascent, the first, that of Judge Wickersham in 1903, and the last, ten years later, are the only ones that have approached their task in this natural and easy way. The others have all burdened themselves with the great and unnecessary difficulties of the southern slopes of the range.

It was proposed to use the mission launch *Pelican*, which has travelled close to twenty thousand miles on the Yukon and its tributaries in the six seasons she has been in commission, to transport the supplies up the Kantishna and Bearpaw Rivers to the head of navigation of the latter, when her cruise of 1912 was complete. But a

Tatum, Esaias, Karstens, Johnny and Walter, at the Clearwater Camp.

serious mishap to the launch, which it was impossible to repair in Alaska, brought her activities for that season to a sudden end. So Mr. Karstens came down from Fairbanks with his launch, and a poling boat loaded with food staples, and, pushing the poling boat ahead, successfully ascended the rivers and carefully cached the stuff some fifty miles from the base of the mountain. It was done in a week or less.

Unfortunately, the equipment and supplies ordered from the outside did not arrive in time to go in with the bulk of the stuff. Although ordered in February, they arrived at Tanana only late in September, just in time to catch the last boat up to Nenana. And only half that had been ordered came at all—one of the two cases has not been traced to this day. Moreover, it was not until late the next February, when actually about to proceed on the expedition, that the writer was able to learn what items had come and what had not. Such are the difficulties of any undertaking in Alaska, despite all the precautions that foresight may dictate.

The silk tents, which had not come, had to be made in Fairbanks; the ice-axes sent were ridiculous gold-painted toys with detachable heads and broomstick handles—more like dwarf halberds than ice-axes; and at least two workmanlike axes were indispensable. So the head of an axe was sawn to the pattern of the writer's out of a piece of tool steel and a substantial hickory handle and an iron shank fitted to it at the machine-shop in Fairbanks. It served excellently well, while the points of the fancy axes from New York splintered the first time they were used. "Climbing-irons," or "crampons," were also to make, no New York dealer being able to supply them.

One great difficulty was the matter of footwear. Heavy regulation-nailed alpine boots were sent—all too small to be worn with even a couple of pairs of socks, and therefore quite useless. Indeed, at that time there was no house in New York, or, so far as the writer knows, in the United States, where the standard alpine equipment could be procured. As a result of the dissatisfaction of this expedition with the material sent, one house in New York now carries in stock a good assortment of such things of standard pattern and quality. Fairbanks was ransacked for boots of any kind in which three or four pairs of socks could be worn. Alaska is a country of big men accustomed to the natural spread of the foot which a moccasin permits, but we could not find boots to our need save rubber snow-packs, and we bought half a dozen pairs of them (No. 12) and had leather soles fastened under them and nailed. Four pairs of alpine boots at eleven dollars a pair equals forty-four dollars. Six pairs of snow-packs at five dollars equals thirty dollars. Leather soles for them at three dollars equals eighteen dollars; which totalled ninety-two dollars—entirely wasted. We found that moccasins were the only practicable foot-gear; and we had to put *five* pairs of socks within them before we were done. But we did not know that at the time and had no means of discovering it.

All these matters were put in hand under Karstens's direction, while the writer, only just arrived in Fairbanks from Fort Yukon and Tanana, made a flying trip to the new mission at the Tanana Crossing, two hundred and fifty miles above Fairbanks, with Walter and the dog team; and most of them were finished by the time we returned. A multitude of small details kept us several days more in Fairbanks, so that nearly the middle of March had arrived before we were ready to make our start to the mountain, two weeks later than we had planned.

Karstens having joined us, we went down to the mission at Nenana (seventy-five miles) in a couple of days, and there two more days were spent overhauling and repacking the stuff that had come from the outside. In the way of food, we had imported only erbswurst, seventy-two four-ounce packages; milk chocolate, twenty pounds; compressed China tea in tablets (a most excellent tea with a very low percentage of tannin), five pounds; a specially selected grade of Smyrna figs, ten pounds; and sugared almonds, ten pounds —about seventy pounds' weight, all scrupulously reserved for the high-mountain work.

For trail equipment we had one eight-by-ten "silk" tent, used for two previous winters; three small circular tents of the same material, made in Fairbanks, for the high work; a Yukon stove and the usual complement of pots and pans and dishes, including two admirable large aluminum pots for melting snow, used a number of years with great satisfaction. A "primus" stove, borrowed from the *Pelican's* galley, was taken along for the high work. The bedding was mainly of down quilts, which are superseding fur robes and blankets for winter use because of their lightness and warmth and the small compass into which they may be compressed. Two pairs of camel's-hair blankets and one sleeping-bag lined with down and camel's-hair cloth were taken, and Karstens brought a

Striking across from the Tanana to the Kantishna.

great wolf-robe, weighing twenty-five pounds, of which we were glad enough later on.

Another team was obtained at the mission, and Mr. R. G. Tatum and the two boys, Johnny and Esaias, joined the company, which, thus increased to six persons, two sleds, and fourteen dogs, set out from Nenana across country to the Kantishna on St. Patrick's day.

Travelling was over the beaten trail to the Kantishna gold camp, one of the smallest of Alaskan camps, supporting about thirty men. In 1906 there was a wild stampede to this region, and two or three thousand people went in, chiefly from the Fairbanks district. Town after town was built—Diamond City, Glacier City, Bearpaw City, Roosevelt, McKinley City—all with elaborate saloons and gambling-places, one, at least, equipped with electric lights. But next summer the boom burst and all the thousands streamed out. Gold there was and is yet, but in small quantities only. The "cities" are mere collections of tumble-down huts amongst which the moose roam at will. Interior Alaska has many such abandoned "cities." The few men now in the district have placer claims that yield a "grub-stake" as a sure thing every summer, and spend their winters chiefly in prospecting for quartz. At Diamond

City, on the Bearpaw, lay our cache of grub, and that place, some ninety miles from Nenana and fifty miles from the base of Denali, was our present objective point. It was bright, clear weather and the trail was good. For thirty miles our way lay across the wide flats of the Tanana Valley, and this stage brought us to the banks of the Nenana River. Another day of twenty-five miles of flats brought us to Knight's comfortable road-house and ranch on the Toklat, a tributary of the Kantishna, the only road-house this trail can now support. Several times during these two days we had clear glimpses of the great mountain we were approaching, and as we came out of the flat country, the "Sheephills," a foot-hill range of Denali, much broken and deeply sculptured, rose picturesquely before us. Our travel was now almost altogether on "overflow" ice, upon the surface of swift streams that freeze solidly over their riffles and shallows and thus deny passage under the ice to the water of fountains and springs that never ceases flowing. So it bursts forth and flows *over* the ice with a continually renewing surface of the smoothest texture. Carrying a mercurial barometer that one dare not intrust to a sled on one's back over such footing is a somewhat precarious proceeding, but there

One of the abandoned mining towns in the Kantishna.

was no alternative, and many miles were thus passed. Up the Toklat, then up its Clearwater Fork, then up its tributary, Myrtle Creek, to its head, and so over a little divide and down Willow Creek, we went, and from that divide and the upper reaches of the last-named creek had fine, clear views not only of Denali but of Denali's Wife as well, now come much nearer and looming much larger.

But here it may be stated once for all that the view which this face of the mountains presents is never a satisfying one. The same is true in even greater degree of the southern face, all photographs agreeing with all travellers as to its tameness. There is only one face of the Denali group that is completely satisfying, that is adequate to the full picturesque potentiality of a twenty-thousand-foot elevation. The writer has seen no other view, no other aspect of it, comparable to that of the northwest face from Lake Minchúmina. There the two mountains rise side by side, sheer, precipitous, pointed rocks, utterly inaccessible, savage, and superb. The rounded shoulders, the receding slopes and ridges of the other faces detract from the uplift and from the dignity, but the northwestern face is stark.

One more run, of much the same character as

the previous day, and we were at Eureka, in the heart of the Kantishna country, on Friday, 21st March, being Good Friday.

We arrived there at noon and "called it a day," and spent the rest of it in the devotions of that august anniversary. Easter eve took us to Glacier City, and we lay there over the feast, gathering three or four men who were operating a prospecting-drill in that neighborhood for the first public worship ever conducted in the Kantishna camp. Ten miles more brought us to Diamond City, on the Bearpaw, where we found our cache of food in good condition save that the field-mice, despite all precautions, had made access to the cereals and had eaten all the rolled oats.

Amongst the Kantishna miners, who were most kindly and generous in their assistance, we were able to pick up enough large-sized moccasins to serve the members of the party, and we wore nothing else at all on the mountain.

Our immediate task now lay before us. A ton and a half of supplies had to be hauled some fifty miles across country to the base of the mountain. Here the relaying began, stuff being taken ahead and cached at some midway point, then another load taken right through a day's march, and then

Denali from the McKinley fork of the Kantishna River.

Showing the two peaks of the mountain, the one in the rear and to the left (the South Peak) is the higher.

a return made to bring up the cache. In this way we moved steadily though slowly across rolling country and upon the surface of a large lake to the McKinley Fork of the Kantishna, which drains the Muldrow Glacier, down that stream to its junction with the Clearwater Fork of the same, and up that fork, through its canyon, to the last spruce timber on its banks, and there we made a camp in an exceedingly pretty spot. The creek ran open through a break in the ice in front of our tent; the water-ousels darted in and out under the ice, singing most sweetly; the willows, all in bud, perfumed the air; and Denali soared clear and brilliant, far above the range, right in front of us. Here at the timber-line, at an elevation of about two thousand feet, was the pleasantest camp of the whole excursion. During the five days' stay here the stuff was brought up and carried forward, and a quantity of dry wood was cut and advanced to a cache at the mouth of the creek by which we should reach the Muldrow Glacier.

It should be said that the short and easy route by which that glacier is reached was discovered after much scouting and climbing by McGonogill and Taylor in 1910, upon the occasion of the "pioneer" attempt upon the mountain, of which more will be said by and by. The men in the

Kantishna camp who took part in that attempt gave us all the information they possessed, as they had done to the party that attempted the mountain last summer. There has been no need to make reconnoissance for routes since these pioneers blazed the way: there is no other practicable route than the one they discovered. The two subsequent climbing parties have followed precisely in their footsteps up as far as the Grand Basin at sixteen thousand feet, and it is the merest justice that such acknowledgment be made.

At our camp the Clearwater ran parallel with the range, which rose like a great wall before us. Our approach was not directly toward Denali but toward an opening in the range six or eight miles to the east of the great mountain. This opening is known as Cache Creek. Passing the willow patch at its mouth, where previous camps had been made, we pushed up the creek some three miles more to its forks, and there established our base camp, on 10th April, at about four thousand feet elevation. A few scrubby willows struggled to grow in the creek bed, but the hills that rose from one thousand five hundred to two thousand feet around us were bare of any vegetation save moss and were yet in the main covered with snow.

Entering the range by Cache Creek.

The Muldrow Glacier flows between the peak in the background (Mt. Brooks) and the ridge just below it.

Caribou signs were plentiful everywhere, and we were no more than settled in camp when a herd appeared in sight.

Our prime concern at this camp was the gathering and preserving of a sufficient meat supply for our subsistence on the mountain. It was an easy task. First Karstens killed a caribou and then Walter a mountain-sheep. Then Esaias happened into the midst of a herd of caribou as he climbed over a ridge, and killed three. That was all we needed. Then we went to work preparing the meat. Why should any one haul canned pemmican hundreds of miles into the greatest game country in the world? We made our own pemmican of the choice parts of this tender, juicy meat and we never lost appetite for it or failed to enjoy and assimilate it. A fifty-pound lard-can, three parts filled with water, was set on the stove and kept supplied with joints of meat. As a batch was cooked we took it out and put more into the same water, removed the flesh from the bones, and minced it. Then we melted a can of butter, added pepper and salt to it, and rolled a handful of the minced meat in the butter and moulded it with the hands into a ball about as large as a baseball. We made a couple of hundred of such balls and froze them, and they kept perfectly.

When all the boiling was done we put in the hocks of the animals and boiled down the liquor into five pounds of the thickest, richest meat-extract jelly, adding the marrow from the bones. With this pemmican and this extract of caribou, a package of erbswurst and a cupful of rice, we concocted every night the stew which was our main food in the higher regions.

Here the instruments were overhauled. The mercurial barometer reading by verniers to three places of decimals was set up and read, and the two aneroids were adjusted to read with it. These two aneroids perhaps deserve a word. Aneroid A was a three-inch, three-circle instrument, the invention of Colonel Watkins, of the British army, of range-finder fame. It seems strange that the advantage of the three-circle aneroid is so little known in this country, for its three concentric circles give such an open scale that, although this particular instrument reads to twenty-five thousand feet, it is easy to read as small a difference as twenty feet on it. It had been carried in the hind sack of the writer's sled for the past eight winters and constantly and satisfactorily used to determine the height of summits and passes upon the trails of the interior. Aneroid B was a six-inch patent mountain ane-

The base-camp at about 4,000 feet on Cache Creek.

The Muldrow Glacier flows between the ridge in the background and the peak just beyond it.

roid, another invention of the same military genius, prompted by Mr. Whymper's experiments with the aneroid barometer after his return from his classic climbs to the summits of the Bolivian Andes. Colonel Watkins devised an instrument in which by a threaded post and a thumb-screw the spring may be relaxed or brought into play at will, and the instrument is never in commission save when a reading is taken. Then a few turns of the thumb-screw bring the spring to bear upon the box, its walls expand until the pressure of the spring equals the pressure of the atmosphere, the reading is taken, and the instrument thrown out of operation again—a most ingenious arrangement by which it was hoped to overcome some of the persistent faults of elastic-chamber barometers. The writer had owned this instrument for the past ten years, but had never opportunity to test its usefulness until now. So, although it read no lower than about fifteen inches, he took it with him to observe its operation. Lastly, completing the hypsometrical equipment, was a boiling-point thermometer, with its own lamp and case, reading to 165° by tenths of a degree.

Then there were the ice-creepers or crampons to adjust to the moccasins—terribly heavy, clumsy rat-trap affairs they looked, but they served us well on the higher reaches of the mountain and are, if not indispensable, at least most valuable where hard snow or ice is to be climbed. The snowshoes, also, had to be rough-locked by lashing a wedge-shaped bar of hardwood underneath, just above the tread, and screwing calks along the sides. Thus armed, they gave us sure footing on soft snow slopes, and were particularly useful in ascending the glacier. While thus occupied at the base camp, came an Indian, his wife and child, all the way from Lake Minchúmina, perhaps one hundred miles' journey, to have the child baptized. It was generally known amongst all the natives of the region that the enterprise was on foot, and "Minchúmina John," hoping to meet us in the Kantishna, and missing us, had followed our trail thus far. It was interesting to speculate how much further he would have penetrated: Walter thought as far as the glacier, but I think he would have followed as far as the dogs could go or until food was quite exhausted.

Meanwhile, the relaying of the supplies and the wood to the base camp had gone on, and the advancing of it to a cache at the pass by which we should gain the Muldrow Glacier. On 15th April Esaias and one of the teams were sent back to Nenana. Almost all the stuff we should move

Some heads of game killed at the base-camp.

was already at this cache, and the need for the two dog teams was over. Moreover, the trails were rapidly breaking up, and it was necessary for the boy to travel by night instead of by day on his return trip. Johnny and the other dog team we kept, because we designed to use the dogs up to the head of the glacier, and the boy to keep the base camp and tend the dogs, when this was done, until our return. So we said good-by to Esaias, and he took out the last word that was received from us in more than two months.

The photograph of the base camp shows a mountainous ridge stretching across much of the background. That ridge belongs to the outer wall of the Muldrow Glacier and indicates its general direction. Just beyond the picture, to the right, the ridge breaks down, and the little valley in the middle distance sweeps around, becomes a steep, narrow gulch, and ends at the breach in the glacier wall. This breach, thus reached, is the pass which the Kantishna miners of the "pioneer" expedition discovered and named "McPhee Pass," after a Fairbanks saloon-keeper. The name should stand. There is no other pass by which the glacier can be reached; certainly none at all above, and probably no convenient one below. Unless this pass were used, it would be necessary to make the long and difficult journey to the snout of the glacier, some twenty miles farther to the east, cross its rough terminal moraine, and traverse all its lower stretch.

On the 11th April Karstens and I wound our way up the narrow, steep defile for about three miles from the base camp and came to our first sight of the Muldrow Glacier, some two thousand five hundred feet above camp and six thousand three hundred feet above the sea. That day stands out in recollection as one of the notable days of the whole ascent. There the glacier stretched away, broad and level—the road to the heart of the mountain, and as our eyes traced its course our spirits leaped up that at last we were entered upon our real task. One of us, at least, knew something of the dangers and difficulties its apparently smooth surface concealed, yet to both of us it had an infinite attractiveness, for it was the highway of desire.

CHAPTER II

THE MULDROW GLACIER

RIGHT opposite McPhee Pass, across the glacier, perhaps at this point half a mile wide, rises a bold pyramidal peak, twelve thousand or thirteen thousand feet high, which we would like to name Mount Farthing, in honor of the memory of a very noble gentlewoman who died at the mission at Nenana three years ago, unless, unknown to us, it already bear some other name.* Walter and our two Indian boys had been under her instruction.

At the base of this peak two branches of the glacier unite, coming down in the same general direction and together draining the snows of the whole eastern face of the mountain. The dividing wall between them, almost up to their head and termination, is one stupendous, well-nigh vertical escarpment of ice-covered rock towering six thousand or seven thousand feet above the glacier

* I have since learned that this mountain was named Mount Brooks by Professor Parker, and so withdraw the suggested name.

floor, the first of the very impressive features of the mountain. The other wall of the glacier, through a breach in which we reached its surface —the right-hand wall as we journeyed up it—consists of a series of inaccessible cliffs deeply seamed with snow gullies and crusted here and there with hanging glaciers, the rock formation changing several times as one proceeds but maintaining an unbroken rampart.

Now, it is important to remember that these two ridges which make the walls of the Muldrow Glacier rise ultimately to the two summits of the mountain, the right-hand wall culminating in the North Peak and the left-hand wall in the South Peak. And the glacier lies between the walls all the way up and separates the summits, with this qualification—that midway in its course it is interrupted by a perpendicular ice-fall of about four thousand feet by which its upper portion discharges into its lower. It will help the reader to a comprehension of the ascent if this rough sketch be borne in mind.

The course of the glacier at the point at which we reached it is nearly northeast and southwest (magnetic); its surface is almost level and it is free of crevasses save at its sides. For three or four miles above the pass it pursues its course

The Muldrow Glacier. Karstens in the foreground.

without change of direction or much increase in grade; then it takes a broad sweep toward the south and grows steep and much crevassed. Three miles farther up it takes another and more decided southerly bend, receiving two steep but short tributaries from the northwest at an elevation of about ten thousand feet, and finishing its lower course in another mile and a half, at an elevation of about eleven thousand five hundred feet, with an almost due north and south direction (magnetic).

A week after our first sight of the glacier, or on the 18th April, we were camped at about the farthest point we had been able to see on that occasion—just round the first bend. Our stuff had been freighted to the pass and cached there; then, in the usual method of our advance, the camp had been moved forward beyond the cache on to the glacier, a full day's march. Then the team worked backward, bringing up the stuff to the new camp. Thus three could go ahead, prospecting and staking out a trail for further advance, while two worked with the dog team at the freighting.

For the glacier difficulties now confronted us in the fullest degree. Immediately above our tent the ice rose steeply a couple of hundred feet, and at that level began to be most intricately crevassed. It took several days to unravel the tangle of fissures and discover and prepare a trail that the dogs could haul the sleds along. Sometimes a bridge would be found over against one wall of the glacier, and for the next we might have to go clear across to the other wall. Sometimes a block of ice jammed in the jaws of a crevasse would make a perfectly safe bridge; sometimes we had nothing upon which to cross save hardened snow. Some of the gaps were narrow and some wide, yawning chasms. Some of them were mere surface cracks and some gave hundreds of feet of deep blue ice with no bottom visible at all. Sometimes there was no natural bridge over a crevasse, and then, choosing the narrowest and shallowest place in it, we made a bridge, excavating blocks of hard snow with the shovels and building them up from a ledge below, or projecting them on the cantilever principle, one beyond the other from both sides. Many of these crevasses could be jumped across by an unencumbered man on his snow-shoes that could not have been jumped with a pack and that the dogs could not cross at all. As each section of trail was determined it was staked out with willow shoots, hundreds of which had been brought up from below. And in all of this pioneering work, and, indeed, thenceforward invariably, the rope was conscientiously used. Every step of the way up the glacier was sounded by a long pole, the man in the lead thrusting it deep into the snow while the two behind kept the rope always taut. More than one pole slipped into a hidden crevasse and was lost when vigor of thrust was not matched by tenacity of grip; more than once a man was jerked back just as the snow gave way beneath his feet. The open crevasses were not the dangerous ones; the whole glacier was crisscrossed by crevasses completely covered with snow. In bright weather it was often possible to detect them by a slight depression in the surface or by a faint, shadowy difference in tint, but in the half-light of cloudy and misty weather these signs failed, and there was no safety but in the ceaseless prodding of the pole. The ice-axe will not serve—one cannot reach far enough forward with it for safety, and the incessant stooping is an unnecessary added fatigue.

For the transportation of our wood and supplies beyond the first glacier camp, the team of six dogs was cut into two teams of three, each drawing a little Yukon sled procured in the Kantishna, the large basket sled having been abandoned. And in the movement forward, when the trail to a convenient cache had been established, two men, roped together, accompanied each sled, one ahead of the dogs, the other just behind the dogs at the gee-pole. This latter had also a hauling-line looped about his breast, so that men and dogs and sled made a unit. It took the combined traction power of men and dogs to take the loads up the steep glacial ascents, and it was very hard work. Once, "Snowball," the faithful team leader of four years past, who has helped to haul my sled nearly ten thousand miles, broke through a snow bridge and, the belly-band parting, slipped out of his collar and fell some twenty feet below to a ledge in a crevasse. Walter was let down and rescued the poor brute, trembling but uninjured. Without the dogs we should have been much delayed and could hardly, one judges, have moved the wood forward at all. The work on the glacier was the beginning of the ceaseless grind which the ascent of Denali demands.

How intolerably hot it was, on some of these days, relaying the stuff up the glacier! I shall never forget Ascension Day, which occurred this year on the 1st May. Double feast as it was—for SS. Philip and James falls on that day—it was a day of toil and penance. With the mercurial barometer and a heavy pack of instruments and

Ascension Day, 1913.

cameras and films on my back and the rope over my shoulder, bent double hauling at the sled, I trudged along all day, panting and sweating, through four or five inches of new-fallen snow, while the glare of the sun was terrific. It seemed impossible that, surrounded entirely by ice and snow, with millions of tons of ice underfoot, it *could* be so hot. But we took the loads right through to the head of the glacier that day, rising some four thousand feet in the course of five miles, and cached them there. On other days a smother of mist lay all over the glacier surface, with never a breath of wind, and the air seemed warm and humid as in an Atlantic coast city in July. Yet again, starting early in the morning, sometimes a zero temperature nipped toes and fingers and a keen wind cut like a knife. Sometimes it was bitterly cold in the mornings, insufferably hot at noon, and again bitterly cold toward night. It was a pity we had no black-bulb, sun-maximum thermometer amongst our instruments, for one is sure its readings would have been of great interest.

It was a pity, also, that we had no means of making an attempt at measuring the rate of movement of this glacier—a subject we often discussed. The carriage of poles enough to set out rows of them across the glacier would have greatly increased our loads and the time required to transport them. But it is certain that its rate of movement is very slow in general, though faster at certain spots than at others, and a reason for this judgment will be given later.

The midway cache between our first and last glacier camps was itself the scene of a camp we had not designed, for on the day we were moving finally forward we were too fatigued to press on to the spot that had been selected at the head of the glacier, and by common consent made a halt at the cache and set up the tent there. This is mentioned because it had consequences. If we had gone through that day and had established ourselves at the selected spot, a disaster that befell us would, in all probability, not have happened; for the next day, instead of moving our camp forward, we relayed some stuff and cached it where the camp would be made, covering the cache with the three small silk tents. Then we sat around awhile and ate our luncheon, and presently went down for another load. Imagine our surprise, upon returning some hours later, to see a column of smoke rising from our cache. All sorts of wild speculations flew through the writer's mind as, in the lead that day, he first

Bridging a crevasse on the Muldrow Glacier.

crested the sérac that gave view of the cache. Had some mysterious climber come over from the other side of the mountain and built a fire on the glacier? Had he discovered our wood and our grub and, perhaps starving, kindled a fire of the one to cook the other? Was there really, then, some access to this face of the mountain from the south? For it is fixed in the mind of the traveller in the north beyond eradication that *smoke* must mean *man.* But ere we had gone much farther the truth dawned upon us that our cache was on fire, and we left the dogs and the sleds and hurried to the spot. Something we were able to save, but not much, though we were in time to prevent the fire from spreading to our far-hauled wood. And the explanation was not far to seek. After luncheon Karstens and the writer had smoked their pipes, and one or the other had thrown a careless match away that had fallen unextinguished upon the silk tents that covered the cache. Presently a little wind had fanned the smouldering fabric into flame, which had eaten down into the pile of stuff below, mostly in wooden cases. All our sugar was gone, all our powdered milk, all our baking-powder, our prunes, raisins, and dried apples, most of our tobacco, a case of pilot bread, a sack full of woollen socks and gloves, another sack full of photographic films—all were burned. Most fortunately, the food provided especially for the high-mountain work had not yet been taken to the cache, and our pemmican, erbswurst, chocolate, compressed tea, and figs were safe. But it was a great blow to us and involved considerable delay at a very unfortunate time. We felt mortification at our carelessness as keenly as we felt regret at our loss. The last thing a newcomer would dream of would be danger from fire on a glacier, but we were not newcomers, and we all knew how ever-present that danger is, more imminent in Alaska in winter than in summer. Our carelessness had brought us nigh to the ruining of the whole expedition. The loss of the films was especially unfortunate, for we were thus reduced to Walter's small camera with a common lens and the six or eight spools of film he had for it.

The next day the final move of the main camp was made, and we established ourselves in the cirque at the head of the Muldrow Glacier, at an elevation of about eleven thousand five hundred feet, more than half-way up the mountain. After digging a level place in the glacier and setting up the tent, a wall of snow blocks was built all round it, and a little house of snow blocks, a regular

Hard work for dogs as well as men on the Muldrow Glacier.

Eskimo igloo, was built near by to serve as a cache. Some details of our camping may be of interest. The damp from the glacier ice had incommoded us at previous camps, coming up through skins and bedding when the tent grew warm. So at this camp we took further precaution. The boxes in which our grub had been hauled were broken up and laid over the whole portion of the floor of the tent where our bed was; over this wooden floor a canvas cover was laid, and upon this the sun-dried hides of the caribou and mountain-sheep we had killed were placed. There was thus a dry bottom for our bedding, and we were not much troubled thenceforward by the rising moisture, although a camp upon the ice is naturally always a more or less sloppy place. The hides were invaluable; heavy as they were, we carried them all the way up.

So soon as we were thus securely lodged, elated when we thought of our advance, but downcast when we recalled our losses, we set ourselves to repair the damage of the fire so far as it was reparable. Walter and Johnny must go all the way down to the base camp and bring up sled-covers out of which to construct tents, must hunt the baggage through for old socks and mitts, and must draw upon what grub had been left for the return journey to the extreme limit it was safe to do so.

Karstens, accustomed to be clean-shaven, had been troubled since our first glacier camp with an affection of the face which he attributed to "ingrowing whiskers," but when many hairs had been plucked out with the tweezers and he was nothing bettered, but rather grew worse and the inflammation spread to neck and temple, it was more correctly attributed to an eczema, or tetter, caused by the glare of the sun. So he was not loath to seclude himself for a few days in the tent while we set about the making of socks and mitts from the camel's-hair lining of the sleeping-bag. Walter's face was also very sore from the sun, his lips in particular being swollen and blistered. So painful did they become that I had to cut lip covers of surgeon's plaster to protect them. Then the boys returned with the sorry gleanings of the base camp, and the business of making two tents from the soiled and torn sled-covers and darning worn-out socks and mittens, was put in hand. Our camp looked like a sweat-shop those days, with its cross-legged tailormen and its litter of snippets. In addition to the six-by-seven tent, three feet six inches high, in which we were to live when we left the glacier, we made a small, conical tent in which to read the instruments on the summit. And all those days the sun shone in a clear sky!

Here, since reference has just been made to the effect of the sun's glare on the face of one member of the party, it may be in place to speak of the perfect eye protection which the amber snow-glasses afforded us. Long experience with blue and smoke-colored glasses upon the trail in spring had led us to expect much irritation of the eyes despite the use of snow-glasses, and we had plentifully provided ourselves with boracic acid and zinc sulphate for eye-washes. But the amber glasses, with their yellow celluloid side-pieces, were not a mere palliative, as all other glasses had been in our experience, but a complete preventive of snow-blindness. No one of us had the slightest trouble with the eyes, and the eye-washes were never used. It is hard for any save men compelled every spring to travel over the dazzling snows to realize what a great boon this newly discovered amber glass is. There is no reason anywhere for any more snow-blindness, and there is no use anywhere for any more blue or smoked glasses. The invention of the amber snow-glass is an even greater blessing to the traveller in the north than the invention of the thermos bottle.

No test could be more severe than that which we put these glasses to.

We were now at the farthest point at which it was possible to use the dogs, at our actual climbing base, and the time had come for Johnny and the dogs to go down to the base camp for good. We should have liked to keep the boy, so good-natured and amiable he was and so keen for further climbing; but the dogs must be tended, and the main food for them was yet to seek on the foot-hills with the rifle. So on 9th May down they went, Tatum and the writer escorting them with the rope past the crevasses as far as the first glacier camp, and then toiling slowly up the glacier again, thankful that it was for the last time. That was one of the sultriest and most sweltering days either of us ever remembered, a moist heat of sun beating down through vapor, with never a breath of breeze—a stifling, stewing day that, with the steep climb added, completely exhausted and prostrated us.

It is important that the reader should be able to see, in his mind's eye, the situation of our camp at the head of the glacier, because to do so is to grasp the simple orography of this face of the mountain, and to understand the route of its ascent, probably the only route by which it can be ascended. Standing beside the tent, facing in the direction we have journeyed, the great highway of the glacier comes to an abrupt end, a cul-de-sac. On the right hand the wall of the glacier towers up, with enormous precipitous cliffs incrusted with hanging ice, to the North Peak of the mountain, eight or nine thousand feet above us. About at right angles to the end of the glacier, and four thousand feet above it, is another glacier, which discharges by an almost perpendicular ice-fall upon the floor of the glacier below.* The left-hand wall of the glacier, described some pages back as a stupendous escarpment of ice-covered rock, breaks rapidly down into a comparatively low ridge, which sweeps to the right, encloses the head of the glacier, and then rises rapidly to the glacier above, and still rises to form the left-hand wall of that glacier, and finally the southern or higher peak of the mountain.

So the upper glacier separates the two great peaks of the mountain and discharges at right angles into the lower glacier. And the walls of the lower glacier sweep around and rise to form the walls of the upper glacier, and ultimately the summits of the mountain. To reach the peaks one must first reach the upper glacier, and the

*See frontispiece.

southern or left-hand wall of the lower glacier, where it breaks down into the ridge that encloses the head of the glacier, is the only possible means by which the upper basin may be reached. This ridge, then, called by Parker and Browne the Northeast Ridge (and we have kept that designation, though with some doubt as to its correctness), presented itself as the next stage in our climb.

Now just before leaving Fairbanks we had received a copy of a magazine containing the account of the Parker-Browne climb, and in that narrative Mr. Browne speaks of this Northeast Ridge as "a steep but practicable snow slope," and prints a photograph which shows it as such. To our surprise, when we first reached the head of the glacier, the ridge offered no resemblance whatever to the description or the photograph. The upper one-third of it was indeed as described, but at that point there was a sudden sharp cleavage, and all below was a jumbled mass of blocks of ice and rock in all manner of positions, with here a pinnacle and there a great gap. Moreover, the floor of the glacier at its head was strewn with enormous icebergs that we could not understand at all. All at once the explanation came to us—"the earthquake"! The Parker-Browne party

The Northeast Ridge shattered by the earthquake in July, 1912.

The earthquake cleavage is plainly shown half-way down the ridge in the background. The Browne Tower is the uppermost point in the picture. The Parker Pass is along its base.

had reported an earthquake which shook the whole base of the mountain on 6th July, 1912, two days after they had come down, and, as was learned later, the seismographic instruments at Washington recorded it as the most severe shock since the San Francisco disturbance of 1906. There could be no doubt that the earthquake had disrupted this ridge. The huge bergs all around us were not the normal discharge of hanging glaciers as we had at first wonderingly supposed; they were the incrustation of ages, maybe, ripped off the rocks and hurled down from the ridge by this convulsion. It was as though, as soon as the Parker-Browne party reached the foot of the mountain, the ladder by which they had ascended and descended was broken up.

What a wonderful providential escape these three men, Parker, Browne, and LeVoy had! They reached a spot within three or four hundred feet of the top of the mountain, struggling gallantly against a blizzard, but were compelled at last to beat a retreat. Again from their seventeen-thousand-foot camp they essayed it, only to be enshrouded and defeated by dense mist. They would have waited in their camp for fair weather had they been provided with food, but their stomachs would not retain the canned pemmican they had carried laboriously aloft, and they were compelled to give up the attempt and descend. So down to the foot of the mountain they went, and immediately they reached their base camp this awful earthquake shattered the ridge and showered down bergs on both the upper and lower glaciers. Had their food served they had certainly remained above, and had they remained above their bodies would be there now. Even could they have escaped the avalanching icebergs they could never have descended that ridge after the earthquake. They would either have been overwhelmed and crushed to death instantly or have perished by starvation. One cannot conceive grander burial than that which lofty mountains bend and crack and shatter to make, or a nobler tomb than the great upper basin of Denali; but life is sweet and all men are loath to leave it, and certainly never men who cling to life had more cause to be thankful.

The difficulty of our task was very greatly increased; that was plain at a glance. This ridge, that the pioneer climbers of 1910 went up at one march with climbing-irons strapped beneath their moccasins, carrying nothing but their flagpole, that the Parker-Browne party surmounted in a few days, relaying their camping stuff and supplies, was to occupy us for three weeks while we hewed a staircase three miles long in the shattered ice.

It was the realization of the earthquake and of what it had done that convinced us that this Muldrow Glacier has a very slow rate of movement. The great blocks of ice hurled down from above lay apparently just where they had fallen almost a year before. At the points of sharp descent, at the turns in its course, at the points where tributary glaciers were received, the movement is somewhat more rapid. We saw some crevasses upon our descent that were not in existence when we went up. But for the whole stretch of it we were satisfied that a very few feet a year would cover its movement. No doubt all the glaciers on this side of the range are much more sluggish than on the other side, where the great precipitation of snow takes place.

We told Johnny to look for us in two weeks. It was thirty-one days ere we rejoined him. For now began the period of suspense, of hope blasted anew nearly every morning, the period of weary waiting for decent weather. With the whole mountain and glacier enveloped in thick mist it was not possible to do anything up above, and day after day this was the condition, varied by high wind and heavy snow. From the inexhaustible cisterns of the Pacific Ocean that vapor was distilled, and ever it rose to these mountains and poured all over them until every valley, every glacier, every hollow, was filled to overflowing. There seemed sometimes to us no reason why the process should not go on forever. The situation was not without its ludicrous side, when one had the grace to see it. Here were four men who had already passed through the long Alaskan winter, and now, when the rivers were breaking and the trees bursting into leaf, the flowers spangling every hillside, they were deliberately pushing themselves up into the winter still, with the long-expected summer but a day's march away.

The tedium of lying in that camp while snow-storm or fierce, high wind forbade adventure upon the splintered ridge was not so great to the writer as to some of the other members of the expedition, for there was always Walter's education to be prosecuted, as it had been prosecuted for three winters on the trail and three summers on the launch, in a desultory but not altogether unsuccessful manner. An hour or two spent in writing from dictation, another hour or two in reading aloud, a little geography and a little history and a little physics made the day pass busily. A pupil is a great resource. Karstens was continually designing and redesigning a motor-boat in which one engine should satisfactorily operate twin screws; Tatum learned the thirty-nine articles by heart; but naval architecture and even controversial divinity palled after a while. The equipment and the supplies for the higher region were gone over again and again, to see that all was properly packed and in due proportion.

As one handled the packages and read and re-read the labels, one was struck by the meagre English of merchandisers and the poor verbal resources of commerce generally. A while ago business dealt hardly with the word "proposition." It was the universal noun. Everything that business touched, however remotely, was a "proposition." When last he was "outside" the writer heard the Nicene creed described as a "tough proposition"; the Vice-President of the United States as a "cold-blooded proposition," and missionaries in Alaska generally as "queer propositions." Now commerce has discovered and appropriated the word "product" and is working it for all it is worth. The coffee in the can calls itself a product. The compressed medicines from London direct you to "dissolve one product" in so much water; the vacuum bottles inform you that since they are a "glass product" they will not guarantee themselves against breakage; the tea tablets and the condensed pea soup affirm the purity of "these products"; the powdered milk is a little more explicit and calls itself a "food product." One feels disposed to agree with Humpty Dumpty, in "Through the Looking-Glass," that when a word is worked as hard as this it ought to be paid extra. One feels that "product" ought to be coming round on Saturday night to collect its overtime. The zwieback amuses one; it is a West-coast "product," and apparently "product" has not yet reached the West coast—it does not so dignify itself. But it urges one, in great letters on every package, to "save the end seals; they are valuable!" Walter finds that by gathering one thousand two hundred of these seals he would be entitled to a "rolled-gold" watch absolutely free! This zwieback was the whole stock of a Yukon grocer purchased when the supply we ordered did not arrive. The writer was reminded of the time when he bought several two-pound packages of rolled oats at a little Yukon store and discovered to his disgust that every package contained a china cup and saucer that must have weighed at least a pound. One can understand the poor Indian being thus deluded into the belief that he is getting his crockery for nothing, but it is hard to understand how the "gift-enterprise" and "premium-package" folly still survives amongst white people—and Indians do not eat zwieback. What sort of people are they who will feverishly purchase and consume one thousand two hundred packages of zwieback in order to get a "rolled-gold" watch for nothing? A sack of corn-meal takes one's eye mainly by the enumeration of the formidable processes which the "product" inside has survived. It is announced proudly as "degerminated, granulated, double kiln-dried, steam-ground"! But why, in the name even of an adulterous and adulterating generation, should rice be "coated with talcum and glucose," as this sack unblushingly confesses? It is all very well to add "remove by washing"; that is precisely what we shall be unable to do. It will take all the time and fuel we have to spare to melt snow for cooking, when one little primus stove serves for all purposes. When we leave this camp there will be no more water for the toilet; we shall have to cleanse our hands with snow and let our faces go. The rice will enter the pot unwashed and will transfer its talcum and glucose to our intestines. Nor is this the case merely on exceptional mountain-climbing expeditions; it is the general rule during the winter throughout Alaska. It takes a long time and a great deal of snow and much wood to produce a pot of water on the winter trail. That "talcum-and-glucose" abomination should be taken up by the Pure Food Law authorities. All the rice that comes to Alaska is so labelled. The stomachs and bowels of dogs and men in the country are doubtless gradually becoming "coated with talcum and glucose."

It was during this period of hope deferred that we began to be entirely without sugar. Perhaps by the ordinary man anywhere, certainly by the ordinary man in Alaska, where it is the rule to include as much sugar as flour in an outfit, deprivation of sugar is felt more keenly than deprivation of any other article of food. We watched the gradual dwindling of our little sack, replenished from the base camp with the few pounds we had reserved for our return journey, with sinking hearts. It was kept solely for tea and coffee. We put no more in the sour dough for hot cakes; we ceased its use on our rice for breakfast; we gave up all sweet messes. Tatum attempted a pudding without sugar, putting vanilla and cinnamon and one knows not what other flavorings in it, in the hope of disguising the absence of sweetness, but no one could eat it and there was much jeering at the cook. Still it dwindled and dwindled. Two spoonfuls to a cup were reduced by common consent to one, and still it went, until at last the day came when there was no more. Our cocoa became useless—we could not drink it without sugar; our consumption of tea and coffee diminished—there was little demand for the second cup. And we all began to long for sweet things. We tried to make a palatable potation from some of our milk chocolate, reserved for the higher work and labelled, "For eating only." The label was accurate; it made a miserable drink, the milk taste entirely lacking, the sweetness almost gone. We speculated how our ancestors got on without sugar when it was a high-priced luxury brought painfully in small quantities from the Orient, and assured one another that it was not a necessary article of diet. At last we all agreed to Karstens's laconic advice, "Forget it!" and we spoke of sugar no more. When we got on the ridge the chocolate satisfied to some extent the craving for sweetness, but we all missed the sugar sorely and continued to miss it to the end, Karstens as much as anybody else.

Our long detention here made us thankful for the large tent and the plentiful wood supply. That wood had been hauled twenty miles and raised nearly ten thousand feet, but it was worth while since it enabled us to "weather out the weather" here in warmth and comparative comfort. The wood no more than served our need; indeed, we had begun to economize closely before we left this camp.

We were greatly interested and surprised at the intrusion of animal life into these regions totally devoid of any vegetation. A rabbit followed us up the glacier to an elevation of ten thousand feet, gnawing the bark from the willow shoots with which the trail was staked, creeping round the crevasses, and, in one place at least, leaping such a gap. At ten thousand feet he turned back and descended, leaving his tracks plain in the snow. We speculated as to what possible object he could have had, and decided that he was migrating from the valley below, overstocked with rabbits as it was, and had taken a wrong direction for his purpose. Unless the ambition for first ascents have reached the leporidæ, this seems the only explanation.

At this camp at the head of the glacier we saw ptarmigan on several occasions, and heard their unmistakable cry on several more, and once we felt sure that a covey passed over the ridge above us and descended to the other glacier. It was always in thick weather that these birds were noticed at the glacier head, and we surmised that perhaps they had lost their way in the cloud.

But even this was not the greatest height at which bird life was encountered. In the Grand Basin, at sixteen thousand five hundred feet, Walter was certain that he heard the twittering of small birds familiar throughout the winter in Alaska, and this also was in the mist. I have never known the boy make a mistake in such matters, and it is not essentially improbable. Doctor Workman saw a pair of choughs at twenty-one thousand feet, on Nun Kun in the Himalayas.

Our situation on the glacier floor, much of the time enveloped in dense mist, was damp and cold and gloomy. The cliffs around from time to time discharged their unstable snows in avalanches that threw clouds of snow almost across the wide glacier. Often we could see nothing, and the noise of the avalanches without the sight of them was at times a little alarming. But the most notable discharges were those from the great ice-fall, and the more important of them were startling and really very grand sights. A slight movement would begin along the side of the ice, in one of the gullies of the rock, a little trickling and rattling. Gathering to itself volume as it descended, it started ice in other gullies and presently there was a roar from the whole face of the enormous hanging glacier, and the floor upon which the precipitation descended trembled and shook with the impact of the discharge. Dense volumes of snow and ice dust rose in clouds thousands of feet high and slowly drifted down the glacier. We had chosen our camping-place to be out of harm's way and were really quite safe. We never saw any large masses detached, and by the time the ice reached the glacier floor it was all reduced to dust and small fragments. One does not recall in the reading of mountaineering books any account of so lofty an ice-fall.

Cutting a staircase three miles long in the ice of the shattered ridge.

CHAPTER III

THE NORTHEAST RIDGE

SOME of the photographs we succeeded in getting will show better than any words the character of the ridge we had to climb to the upper basin by. The lowest point of the ridge was that nearest our camp. To reach its crest at that point, some three hundred feet above the glacier, was comparatively easy, but when it was reached there stretched ahead of us miles and miles of ice-blocks heaved in confusion, resting at insecure angles, poised, some on their points, some on their edges, rising in this chaotic way some 3,000 feet. Here one would have to hew steps up and over a pinnacle, there one must descend again and cut around a great slab. Our wisest course was to seek to reach the crest of the ridge much further along, beyond as much of this ice chaos as possible. But it was three days before we could find a way of approach to the crest that did not take us under overhanging icebergs that threatened continually to fall upon our heads, as the overhanging hill threatened Christian in the "Pilgrim's Progress." At last we took straight up a steep gully, half of it snow slope, the upper half ice-incrusted rock, and hewed steps all the five hundred feet to the top. Here we were about half a mile beyond the point at which we first attained the crest, with that half mile of ice-blocks cut out, but beyond us the prospect loomed just as difficult and as dangerous. We could cut out no more of the ridge; we had tried place after place and could reach it safely at no point further along. The snow slopes broke off with the same sharp cleavage the whole ridge displayed two thousand five hundred feet above; there was no other approach.

So our task lay plain and onerous, enormously more dangerous and laborious than that which our predecessors encountered. We must cut steps in those ice-blocks, over them, around them, on the sheer sides of them, under them—whatever seemed to our judgment the best way of circumventing each individual block. Every ten yards presented a separate problem. Here was a sharp black rock standing up in a setting of ice as thin and narrow and steep as the claws that hold the stone in a finger-ring. That ice must be chopped down level, and then steps cut all round the rock. It took a solid hour to pass that rock. Here was a great bluff of ice, with snow so loose and at such a sharp angle about it that passage had to be hewed up and over and down it again. On either side the ridge fell precipitously to a glacier floor, with yawning crevasses half-way down eagerly swallowing every particle of ice and snow that our axes dislodged: on the right hand to the west fork of the Muldrow Glacier, by which we had journeyed hither; on the left to the east fork of the same, perhaps one thousand five hundred feet, perhaps two thousand feet lower. At the gap in the ridge, with the ice gable on the other side of it, the difficulty and the danger were perhaps at their greatest. It took the best part of a day's cutting to make steps down the slope and then straight up the face of the enormous ice mass that confronted us. The steps had to be made deep and wide; it was not merely one passage we were making; these steps would be traversed again and again by men with heavy packs as we relayed our food and camp equipage along this ridge, and we were determined from the first to take no unnecessary risks whatever. We realized that the passage of this shattered ridge was an exceedingly risky thing at best. To go along it day after day seemed like tempting Providence. We were resolved that nothing on our part should be lacking that could contribute to safety. Day by day we advanced a little further and returned to camp.

The weather doubled the time and the tedium of the passage of this ridge. From Whitsunday to Trinity Sunday, inclusive, there were only two days that we could make progress on the ridge at all, and on one of those days the clouds from the coast poured over so densely and enveloped us so completely that it was impossible to see far enough ahead to lay out a course wisely. On that day we toppled over into the abyss a mass of ice, as big as a two-story house, that must have weighed hundreds of tons. It was poised upon two points of another ice mass and held upright by a flying buttress of wind-hardened snow. Three or four blows from Karstens's axe sent it hurling downward. It passed out of our view into the cloud-smother immediately, but we heard it bound and rebound until it burst with a report like a cannon, and some days later we saw its fragments strewn all over the flat two thousand feet below. What a sight it must have been last July, when the whole ridge was heaving, shattering, and showering down its bergs upon the glacier floors! One day we were driven off the ridge by a high wind that threatened to sweep

The shattered Northeast Ridge.

us from our footholds. On another, a fine morning gave place to a sudden dense snow-storm that sent us quickly below again. Always all day long, while we were on that ridge, the distant thunder of avalanches resounded from the great basin far above us, into which the two summits of Denali were continually discharging their snows. It sounded as though the King of Denmark were drinking healths all day long to the salvoes of his artillery—that custom "more honored in the breach than in the observance." From such fancy the mind passed easily enough to the memory of that astonishing composition of Grieg's, "In the Hall of the Mountain King," and, once recalled, the stately yet staccato rhythm ran in one's ears continually. For if we had many days of cloud and smother of vapor that blotted out everything, when a fine day came how brilliant beyond all that lower levels know it was! From our perch on that ridge the lofty peaks and massive ridges rose on every side. As little by little we gained higher and higher eminence the view broadened, and ever new peaks and ridges thrust themselves into view. We were within the hall of the mountain kings indeed; kings nameless here, in this multitude of lofty summits, but that elsewhere in the world would have each one his name and story.

And how eager and impatient we were to rise high enough, to progress far enough on that ridge that we might gaze into the great basin itself from which the thunderings came, the spacious hall of the two lords paramount of all the mountains of the continent—the north and south peaks of Denali! Our hearts beat high with the anticipation not only of gazing upon it but of entering it and pitching our tent in the midst of its august solitudes. To come down again—for there was as yet no spot reached on that splintered backbone where we might make a camp—to pass day after day in our tent on the glacier floor waiting for the bad weather to be done that we might essay it again; to watch the tantalizing and, as it seemed, meaningless fluctuations of the barometer for encouragement; to listen to the driving wind and the swirling snow, how tedious that was!

At last when we had been camped for three weeks at the head of the glacier, losing scarce an hour of usable weather, but losing by far the greater part of the time, when the advance party the day before had reached a tiny flat on the ridge where they thought camp could be made, we took a sudden desperate resolve to move to the ridge at any cost. All the camp contained that would be needed above was made up quickly into four packs, and we struck out, staggering under our loads. Before we reached the first slope of the ridge each man knew in his heart that we were attempting altogether too much. Even Karstens, who had packed his "hundred and a quarter" day after day over the Chilkoot Pass in 1897, admitted that he was "heavy." But we were saved the chagrin of acknowledging that we had undertaken more than we could accomplish, for before we reached the steep slope of the ridge a furious snow-storm had descended upon us and we were compelled to return to camp. The next day we proceeded more wisely. We took up half the stuff and dug out a camping-place and pitched the little tent. Every step had to be shovelled out, for the previous day's snow had filled it, as had happened so many times before, and it took five and one-half hours to reach the new camping-place. On Sunday, 25th May, the first Sunday after Trinity, we took up the rest of the stuff, and established ourselves at a new climbing base, about thirteen thousand feet high and one thousand five hundred feet above the glacier floor, not to descend again until we descended for good.

We were now much nearer our work and it progressed much faster, although as the ridge rose it became steeper and steeper and even more rugged and chaotic, and the difficulty and danger of its passage increased. Our situation up here was decidedly pleasanter than below. We had indeed exchanged our large tent for a small one in which we could sit upright but could not stand, and so narrow that the four of us, lying side by side, had to make mutual agreement to turn over; our comfortable wood-stove for the little kerosene stove; yet when the clouds cleared we had a noble, wide prospect and there was not the sense of damp immurement that the floor of the glacier gave. The sun struck our tent at 4.30 A. M., which is nearly two and one-half hours earlier than we received his rays below, and lingered with us long after our glacier camp was in the shadow of the North Peak. Moreover, instead of being colder, as we expected, it was warmer, the minimum ranging around zero instead of around 10° below.

The rapidity with which the weather changed up here was a continual source of surprise to us. At one moment the skies would be clear, the peaks and the ridge standing out with brilliant definition; literally five minutes later they would be all blotted out by dense volumes of vapor that poured over from the south. Perhaps ten minutes

Camp at 13,000 feet on Northeast Ridge.

more and the cloud had swept down upon the glacier and all above would be clear again; or it might be the vapor deepened and thickened into a heavy snow-storm. Sometimes everything below was visible and nothing above, and a few minutes later everything below would be obscured and everything above revealed.

This great crescent range is, indeed, our rampart against the hateful humidity of the coast and gives to us in the interior the dry, windless, exhilarating cold that is characteristic of our winters. We owe it mainly to this range that our snowfall averages about six feet instead of the thirty or forty feet that falls on the coast. The winds that sweep northward toward this mountain range are saturated with moisture from the warm waters of the Pacific Ocean; but contact with the lofty colds condenses the moisture into clouds and precipitates most of it on the southern slopes as snow. Still bearing all the moisture their lessened temperature will allow, the clouds pour through every notch and gap in the range and press resolutely onward and downward, streaming along the glaciers toward the interior. But all the time of their passage they are parting with their moisture, for the snow is falling from them continually in their course. They reach the interior, indeed, and spread out triumphant over the lowlands, but most of their burden has been deposited along the way. One is reminded of the government train of mules from Fort Egbert that used to supply the remote posts of the "strategic" telegraph line before strategy yielded to economy and the useless line was abandoned. When the train reached the Tanana Crossing it had eaten up nine-tenths of its original load, and only one-tenth remained for the provisioning of the post. So these clouds were being squeezed like a sponge; every saddle they pushed through squeezed them; every peak and ridge they surmounted squeezed them; every glacier floor they crept down squeezed them, and they reached the interior valleys attenuated, depleted, and relatively harmless.

The aneroids had kept fairly well with the mercurial barometer and the boiling-point thermometer until we moved to the ridge; from this time they displayed a progressive discrepancy therewith that put them out of serious consideration, and one was as bad as the other. Eleven thousand feet seemed the limit of their good behavior. To set them back day by day, like Captain Cuttle's watch, would be to depend wholly upon the other instruments anyway, and this is just what we did, not troubling to adjust them. They were read and recorded merely because that routine had been established. Says Burns:

> "There was a lad was born in Kyle,
> But whatna' day o' whatna' style,
> I doubt it's hardly worth the while
> To be sae nice wi' Robin."

So they were just aneroids: aluminum cases, jewelled movements, army-officer patented improvements, Kew certificates, import duty, and all—just aneroids, and one was as bad as the other. Within their limitations they are exceedingly useful instruments, but it is folly to depend on them for measuring great heights.

Perched up here, the constant struggle of the clouds from the humid south to reach the interior was interesting to watch, and one readily understood that Denali and his lesser companions are a prime factor in the climate of interior Alaska.

Day by day Karstens and Walter would go up and resume the finding and making of a way, and Tatum and the writer would relay the stuff from the camp to a cache, some five hundred feet above, and thence to another. The grand objective point toward which the advance party was working was the earthquake cleavage—a clean, sharp cut in the ice and snow of fifty feet in height. Above that point all was smooth, though fearfully steep;

below was the confusion the earthquake had wrought. Each day Karstens felt sure they would reach the break, but each day as they advanced toward it the distance lengthened and the intricate difficulties increased. More than once a passage painfully hewn in the solid ice had to be abandoned, because it gave no safe exit, and some other passage found. At last the cleavage was reached, and it proved the most ticklish piece of the whole ridge to get around. Just below it was a loose snow slope at a dangerous angle, where it seemed only the initial impulse was needed for an avalanche to bear it all below. And just before crossing that snow slope was a wall of overhanging ice beneath which steps must be cut for one hundred yards, every yard of which endangered the climber by disputing the passage of the pack upon his shoulders.

Late in the evening of the 27th May, looking up the ridge upon our return from relaying a load to the cache, we saw Karstens and Walter standing, clear-cut, against the sky, upon the surface of the unbroken snow *above* the earthquake cleavage. Tatum and I gave a great shout of joy, and, far above as they were, they heard us and waved their response. We watched them advance upon the steep slope of the ridge until the usual cloud

A dangerous passage.

descended and blotted them out. The way was clear to the top of the ridge now, and that night our spirits were high, and congratulations were showered upon the victorious pioneers. The next day, when they would have gone on to the pass, the weather drove them back. On that smooth, steep, exposed slope a wind too high for safety beat upon them, accompanied by driving snow. That day a little accident happened that threatened our whole enterprise—on such small threads do great undertakings hang. The primus stove is an admirable device for heating and cooking—superior, one thinks, to all the newfangled "alcohol utilities"—but it has a weak point. The fine stream of kerosene—which, under pressure from the air-pump, is impinged against the perforated copper cup, heated to redness by burning alcohol, and is thus vaporized—first passes through several convolutions of pipe within the burner, and then issues from a hole so fine that some people would not call it a hole at all but an orifice or something like that. That little hole is the weak spot of the primus stove. Sometimes it gets clogged, and then a fine wire mounted upon some sort of handle must be used to dislodge the obstruction. Now, the worst thing that can happen to a primus stove is to get the wire pricker broken off in the burner hole, and that is what happened to us. Without a special tool that we did not possess, it is impossible to get at that burner to unscrew it, and without unscrewing it the broken wire cannot be removed. Tatum and I turned the stove upside down and beat upon it and tapped it, but nothing would dislodge that wire. It looked remarkably like no supper; it looked alarmingly like no more stove. How we wished we had brought the other stove from the launch, also! Every bow on an undertaking of this kind should have two strings. But when Karstens came back he went to work at once, and this was one of the many occasions when his resourcefulness was of the utmost service. With a file, and his usual ingenuity, he constructed, out of the spoon-bowl of a pipe cleaner the writer had in his pocket, the special tool necessary to grip that little burner, and soon the burner was unscrewed and the broken wire taken out and the primus was purring away merrily again, melting the water for supper. We feel sure that we would have pushed on even had we been without fire. The pemmican was cooked already, and could be eaten as it was, and one does not die of thirst in the midst of snow; but calm reflection will hardly allow that we could have reached the summit had we been deprived of all means of cooking and heating.

On this ridge the dough refused to sour, and since our baking-powder was consumed in the fire we were henceforth without bread. A cold night killed the germ in the sour dough, and we were never again able to set up a fermentation in it. Doubtless the air at this altitude is free from the necessary spores or germs of ferment. Pasteur's and Tyndall's experiments on the Alps, which resulted in the overthrow of the theory of spontaneous generation, and the rehabilitation of the old dogma that life comes only from life, were recalled with interest, but without much satisfaction. We tried all sorts of ways of cooking the flour, but none with any success. Next to the loss of sugar we felt the loss of bread, and in the food longings that overtook us bread played a large part.

On Friday, 30th May, the way had been prospected right up to the pass which gives entrance to the Grand Basin; a camping-place had been dug out there and a first load of stuff carried through and cached. So on that morning we broke camp, and the four of us, roped together, began the most important advance we had made yet. With stiff packs on our backs we toiled up the steps that had been cut with so much pains and stopped at the cache just below the cleavage to add yet further burdens. All day nothing was visible beyond our immediate environment. Again and again one would have liked to photograph the sensational-looking traverse of some particularly difficult ice obstacle, but the mist enveloped everything.

Just before we reached the smooth snow slope above the range of the earthquake disturbance lay one of the really dangerous passages of the climb.

It is easier to describe the difficulty and danger of this particular portion of the ascent than to give a clear impression to a reader of other places almost as hazardous. Directly below the earthquake cleavage was an enormous mass of ice, detached from the cleavage wall. From below, it had seemed connected with that wall, and much time and toil had been expended in cutting steps up it and along its crest, only to find a great gulf fixed; so it was necessary to pass along its base. Now from its base there fell away at an exceedingly sharp angle, scarcely exceeding the angle of repose, a slope of soft, loose snow, and the very top of that slope where it actually joined the wall of ice offered the only possible passage. The wall was in the main perpendicular, and turned at a right angle midway. Just where it turned, a great mass bulged out and overhung. This traverse was so long that with both ropes joined it was still necessary for three of the four members of the party to be on the snow slope at once, two men out of sight of the others. Any one familiar with Alpine work will realize immediately the great danger of such a traverse. There was, however, no avoiding it, or, at whatever cost, we should have done so. Twice already the passage had been made by Karstens and Walter, but not with heavy packs, and one man was always on ice while the other was on snow. This time all four must pass, bearing all that men could bear. Cautiously the first man ventured out, setting foot exactly where foot had been set before, the three others solidly anchored on the ice, paying out the rope and keeping it taut. When all the first section of rope was gone, the second man started, and when, in turn, his rope was paid out, the third man started, leaving the last man on the ice holding to the rope. This, of course, was the most dangerous part of this passage. If one of the three had slipped it would have been almost impossible for the others to hold him, and if he had pulled the others down, it would have been quite impossible for the solitary man on the ice to have withstood the strain. When the first man reached solid ice again there was another equally dangerous minute or two, for then all three behind him were on the snow slope. The beetling cliff, where the trail turned at right angles, was the acutely dangerous spot. With heavy and bulky packs it was exceedingly difficult to squeeze past this projection. Ice gives no such entrance to the point of the axe as hard snow does, yet the only aid in steadying the climber, and in somewhat relieving his weight on the loose snow, was afforded by such purchase upon the ice-wall, shoulder high, as that point could effect. Not a word was spoken by any one; all along the ice-wall rang in the writer's ears that preposterous line from "The Hunting of the Snark"—"Silence, not even a shriek!" It was with a deep and thankful relief that we found ourselves safely across, and when a few minutes later we had climbed the steep snow that lay against the cleavage wall and were at last upon the smooth, unbroken crest of the ridge, we realized that probably the worst place in the entire climb was behind us.

Steep to the very limit of climbability as that ridge was, it was the easiest going we had had since we left the glacier floor. The steps were already cut; it was only necessary to lift one foot after the other and set the toe well in the hole, with the ice-axe buried afresh in the snow above at every step. But each step meant the lifting not only of oneself but of one's load, and the increasing altitude, perhaps aggravated by the dense vapor with which the air was charged, made the advance exceedingly fatiguing. From below, the foreshortened ridge seemed only of short length and of moderate grade, could we but reach it—a tantalizingly easy passage to the upper glacier it looked as we chopped our way, little by little, nearer and nearer to it. But once upon it, it lengthened out endlessly, the sky-line always just a little above us, but never getting any closer.

Just before reaching the steepest pitch of the ridge, where it sweeps up in a cock's comb,* we came upon the vestiges of a camp made by our predecessors of a year before, in a hollow dug in the snow—an empty biscuit carton and a raisin package, some trash and brown paper and discolored snow—as fresh as though they had been left yesterday instead of a year ago. Truly the terrific storms of this region are like the storms of Guy Wetmore Carryl's clever rhyme that "come early and avoid the *rush*." They will sweep a man off his feet, as once threatened to our advance party, but will pass harmlessly over a cigarette

*See illustration facing p. 40

stump and a cardboard box; our tent in the glacier basin, ramparted by a wall of ice-blocks as high as itself, we found overwhelmed and prostrate upon our return, but the willow shoots with which we had staked our trail upon the glacier were all standing.

Long as it was, the slope was ended at last, and we came straight to the great upstanding granite slabs amongst which is the natural camping-place in the pass that gives access to the Grand Basin. We named that pass the Parker Pass, and the rock tower of the ridge that rises immediately above it, the most conspicuous feature of this region from below, we named the Browne Tower. The Parker-Browne party was the first to camp at this spot, for the astonishing "sourdough" pioneers made no camp at all above the low saddle of the ridge (as it then existed), but took all the way to the summit of the North Peak in one gigantic stride. The names of Parker and Browne should surely be permanently associated with this mountain they were so nearly successful in climbing, and we found no better places to name for them.

There is only one difficulty about the naming of this pass; strictly speaking, it is not a pass at all, and the writer does not know of any mountaineering term that technically describes it. Yet it

The Upper Basin reached at last. Our camp at the Parker Pass at 15,000 feet.

should bear a name, for it is the doorway to the upper glacier, through which all those who would reach the summit must enter. On the one hand rises the Browne Tower, with the Northeast Ridge sweeping away beyond it toward the South Peak. On the other hand, the ice of the upper glacier plunges to its fall. The upstanding blocks of granite on a little level shoulder of the ridge lead around to the base of the cliffs of the Northeast Ridge, and it is around the base of those cliffs that the way lies to the midst of the Grand Basin. So the Parker Pass we call it and desire that it should be named.

And while names are before us, the writer would ask permission to bestow another. Having nothing to his credit in the matter at all, as the narrative has already indicated, he feels free to say that in his opinion the conquest of the difficulties of the earthquake-shattered ridge was an exploit that called for high qualities of judgment and cautious daring, and would, he thinks, be considered a brilliant piece of mountaineering anywhere in the world. He would like to name that ridge Karstens Ridge, in honor of the man who, with Walter's help, cut that staircase three miles long amid the perilous complexities of its chaotic ice-blocks.

When we reached the Parker Pass all the world

beneath us was shrouded in dense mist, but all above us was bathed in bright sunshine. The great slabs of granite were like a gateway through which the Grand Basin opened to our view.

The ice of the upper glacier, which fills the Grand Basin, came terracing down from some four thousand feet above us and six miles beyond us, with progressive leaps of jagged blue sérac between the two peaks of the mountain, and, almost at our feet, fell away with cataract curve to its precipitation four thousand feet below us. Across the glacier were the sheer, dark cliffs of the North Peak, soaring to an almost immediate summit twenty thousand feet above the sea; on the left, in the distance, was just visible the receding snow dome of the South Peak, with its two horns some five hundred feet higher. The mists were passing from the distant summits, curtain after curtain of gauze draping their heads for a moment and sweeping on.

We made our camp between the granite slabs on the natural camping site that offered itself, and a shovel and an empty alcohol-can proclaimed that our predecessors of last year had done the same.

The next morning the weather had almost completely cleared, and the view below us burst upon our eyes as we came out of the tent into the still air.

The Parker Pass is the most splendid coigne of vantage on the whole mountain, except the summit itself. From an elevation of something more than fifteen thousand feet one overlooks the whole Alaskan range, and the scope of view to the east, to the northeast, and to the southeast is uninterrupted. Mountain range rises beyond mountain range, until only the snowy summits are visible in the great distance, and one knows that beyond the last of them lies the open sea. The near-by peaks and ridges, red with granite or black with shale and gullied from top to bottom with snow and ice, the broad highways of the glaciers at their feet carrying parallel moraines that look like giant tram-lines, stand out with vivid distinction. A lofty peak, that we suppose is Mount Hunter, towers above the lesser summits. The two arms of the Muldrow Glacier start right in the foreground and reveal themselves from their heads to their junction and then to the terminal snout, receiving their groaning tributaries from every evacuating height. The dim blue lowlands, now devoid of snow, stretch away to the northeast, with threads of stream and patches of lake that still carry ice along their banks.

And all this splendor and diversity yielded itself up to us at once; that was the most sensational and spectacular feature of it. We went to sleep in a smother of mist; we had seen nothing as we climbed; we rose to a clear, sparkling day. The clouds were mysteriously rolling away from the lowest depths; the last wisps of vapor were sweeping over the ultimate heights. Here one would like to camp through a whole week of fine weather could such a week ever be counted upon. Higher than any point in the United States, the top of the Browne Tower probably on a level with the top of Mount Blanc, it is yet not so high as to induce the acute breathlessness from which the writer suffered, later, upon any exertion. The climbing of the tower, the traversing to the other side of it, the climbing of the ridge, would afford pleasant excursions, while the opportunity for careful though difficult photography would be unrivalled. Even in thick weather the clouds are mostly below; and their rapid movement, the kaleidoscopic changes which their coming and going, their thickening and thinning, their rising and falling produce, are a never-failing source of interest and pleasure. The changes of light and shade, the gradations of color, were sometimes wonderfully delicate and charming. Seen through

Above all the range except Denali and Denali's Wife.

rapidly attenuating mist, the bold crags of the icy ridge between the glacier arms in the foreground would give a soft French gray that became a luminous mauve before it sprang into dazzling black and white in the sunshine. In the sunshine, indeed, the whole landscape was hard and brilliant, and lacked half-tones, as in the main it lacked color; but when the vapor drew the gauze of its veil over it there came rich, soft, elusive tints that were no more than hinted ere they were gone.

Here, with nothing but rock and ice and snow around, nine thousand feet above any sort of vegetation even in the summer, it was of interest to remember that at the same altitude in the Himalayas good crops of barley and millet are raised and apples are grown, while at a thousand feet or so lower the apricot is ripened on the terrace-gardens.

Karstens and Walter had brought up a load each on their reconnoissance trip; four heavy loads had been brought the day before. There were yet two loads to be carried up from the cache below the cleavage, and Tatum and Walter, always ready to take the brunt of it, volunteered to bring them. So down that dreadful ridge once more the boys went, while Karstens and the writer prospected ahead for a route into the Grand Basin.

The storms and snows of ten or a dozen winters may make a "steep but practicable snow slope" of the Northeast Ridge again. One winter only had passed since the convulsion that disrupted it, and already the snow was beginning to build up its gaps and chasms. All the summer through, for many hours on clear days, the sun will melt those snows and the frost at night will glaze them into ice. The more conformable ice-blocks will gradually be cemented together, while the fierce winds that beat upon the ridge will wear away the supports of the more egregious and unstable blocks, and one by one they will topple into the abyss on this side or on that. It will probably never again be the smooth, homogeneous slope it has been; "the gable" will probably always present a wide cleft, but the slopes beyond it, stripped now of their accumulated ice so as to be unclimbable, may build up again and give access to the ridge.

The point about one thousand five hundred feet above the gable, where the earthquake cleavage took place, will perhaps remain the crux of the climb. The ice-wall rises forty or fifty feet sheer, and the broken masses below it are especially difficult and precipitous, but with care and time and pains it can be surmounted even as we surmounted it. And wind and sun and storm may mollify the forbidding abruptness of even this break in the course of time.

With the exception of this ridge, Denali is not a mountain that presents special mountaineering difficulties of a technical kind. Its difficulties lie in its remoteness, its size, the great distances of snow and ice its climbing must include the passage of, the burdens that must be carried over those distances. We estimated that it was twenty miles of actual linear distance from the pass by which we reached the Muldrow Glacier to the summit. In the height of summer its snow-line will not be higher than seven thousand feet, while at the best season for climbing it, the spring, the snow-line is much lower. Its climbing is, like nearly all Alaskan problems, essentially one of transportation. But the Northeast Ridge, in its present condition, adds all the spice of sensation and danger that any man could desire.

CHAPTER IV

THE GRAND BASIN

THE reader will perhaps be able to sympathize with the feeling of elation and confidence which came to us when we had surmounted the difficulties of the ridge and had arrived at the entrance to the Grand Basin. We realized that the greater and more arduous part of our task was done and that the way now lay open before us. For so long a time this point had been the actual goal of our efforts, for so long a time we had gazed upward at it with hope deferred, that its final attainment was accompanied with no small sense of triumph and gratification and with a great accession of faith that we should reach the top of the mountain.

The ice of the glacier that fills the basin was hundreds of feet beneath us at the pass, but it rises so rapidly that by a short traverse under the cliffs of the ridge we were able to reach its surface and select a camping site thereon at about sixteen thousand feet. It was bitterly cold, with a keen wind that descended in gusts from the heights, and the slow movement of step-cutting gave the man in the rear no opportunity of warming up. Toes and fingers grew numb despite multiple socks within mammoth moccasins and thick gloves within fur mittens.

From this time, during our stay in the Grand Basin and until we had left it and descended again, the weather progressively cleared and brightened until all clouds were dispersed. From time to time there were fresh descents of vapor, and even short snow-storms, but there was no general enveloping of the mountain again. Cold it was, at times even in the sunshine, with "a nipping and an eager air," but when the wind ceased it would grow intensely hot. On the 4th June, at 3 P. M., the thermometer in the full sunshine rose to 50° F.—the highest temperature recorded on the whole excursion—and the fatigue of packing in that thin atmosphere with the sun's rays reflected from ice and snow everywhere was most exhausting. We were burned as brown as Indians; lips and noses split and peeled in spite of continual applications of lanoline, but, thanks to those most beneficent amber snow-glasses, no one of the party had the slightest trouble with his eyes. At night it was always cold, 10° below zero being the highest minimum during our stay in the Grand Basin, and 21° below zero the lowest. But we always slept warm; with sheep-skins and caribou-skins under us, and down quilts and camel's-hair blankets and a wolf-robe for bedding, the four of us lay in that six-by-seven tent, in one bed, snug and comfortable. It was disgraceful overcrowding, but it was warm. The fierce little primus stove, pumped up to its limit and perfectly consuming its kerosene fuel, shot out its corona of beautiful blue flame and warmed the tight, tiny tent. The primus stove, burning seven hours on a quart of coal-oil, is a little giant for heat generation. If we had had two, so that one could have served for cooking and one for heating, we should not have suffered from the cold at all, but as it was, whenever the stew-pot went on the stove, or a pot full of ice to melt, the heat was immediately absorbed by the vessel and not distributed through the tent. But another primus stove would have been another five or six pounds to pack, and we were "heavy" all the time as it was.

Something has already been said about the fatigue of packing, and one would not weary the reader with continual reference thereto; yet it is certain that those who have carried a pack only on the lower levels cannot conceive how enor-

Traverse under the cliffs of the Northeast Ridge to enter the Grand Basin.

mously greater the labor is at these heights. As one rises and the density of the air is diminished, so, it would seem, the weight of the pack or the effect of the weight of the pack is in the same ratio increased. We probably moved from three hundred to two hundred and fifty pounds, decreasing somewhat as food and fuel were consumed, each time camp was advanced in the Grand Basin. We could have done with a good deal less as it fell out, but this we did not know, and we were resolved not to be defeated in our purpose by lack of supplies. But the packing of these loads, relaying them forward, and all the time steeply rising, was labor of the most exhausting and fatiguing kind, and there is no possible way in which it may be avoided in the ascent of this mountain. To roam over glaciers and scramble up peaks free and untrammelled is mountaineering in the Alps. Put a forty-pound pack on a man's back, with the knowledge that to-morrow he must go down for another, and you have mountaineering in Alaska. In the ascent of this twenty-thousand-foot mountain every member of the party climbed at least sixty thousand feet. It is this going down and doing it all over again that is the heart-breaking part of climbing.

It was in the Grand Basin that the writer began

to be seriously affected by the altitude, to be disturbed by a shortness of breath that with each advance grew more distressingly acute. While at rest he was not troubled; mere existence imposed no unusual burden, but even a slight exertion would be followed by a spell of panting, and climbing with a pack was interrupted at every dozen or score of steps by the necessity of stopping to regain breath. There was no nausea or headache or any other symptom of "mountain sickness." Indeed, it is hard for us to understand that affection as many climbers describe it. It has been said again and again to resemble seasickness in all its symptoms. Now the writer is of the unfortunate company that are seasick on the slightest provocation. Even rough water on the wide stretches of the lower Yukon, when a wind is blowing upstream and the launch is pitching and tossing, will give him qualms. But no one of the four of us had any such feeling on the mountain at any time. Shortness of breath we all suffered from, though none other so acutely as myself. When it was evident that the progress of the party was hindered by the constant stops on my account, the contents of my pack were distributed amongst the others and my load reduced to the mercurial barometer and the instruments,

First camp in the Grand Basin—16,000 feet, looking up.

and, later, to the mercurial barometer alone. It was some mortification not to be able to do one's share of the packing, but there was no help for it, and the other shoulders were young and strong and kindly.

With some hope of improving his wind, the writer had reduced his smoking to two pipes a day so soon as the head of the glacier had been reached, and had abandoned tobacco altogether when camp was first made on the ridge; but it is questionable if smoking in moderation has much or any effect. Karstens, who smoked continually, and Walter, who had never smoked in his life, had the best wind of the party. It is probably much more a matter of age. Karstens was a man of thirty-two years, and the two boys were just twenty-one, while the writer approached fifty. None of us slept as well as usual except Walter—and nothing ever interferes with his sleep—but, although our slumbers were short and broken, they seemed to bring recuperation just as though they had been sound. We arose fresh in the morning though we had slept little and light.

On the 30th May we had made our camp at the Parker Pass; on the 2d June, the finest and brightest day in three weeks, we moved to our first camp in the Grand Basin. On the 3d June we moved camp again, out into the middle of the glacier, at about sixteen thousand five hundred feet.

Here we were at the upper end of one of the flats of the glacier that fills the Grand Basin, the sérac of another great rise just above us. The walls of the North Peak grow still more striking and picturesque here, where they attain their highest elevation. These granite ramparts, falling three thousand feet sheer, swell out into bellying buttresses with snow slopes between them as they descend to the glacier floor, while on top, above the granite, each peak point and crest ridge is tipped with black shale. How comes that ugly black shale, with the fragments of which all the lower glacier is strewn, to have such lofty eminence and granite-guarded distinction, as though it were the most beautiful or the most valuable thing in the world? The McKinley Fork of the Kantishna, which drains the Muldrow, is black as ink with it, and its presence can be detected in the Tanana River itself as far as its junction with the Yukon. It is largely soluble in water, and where melting snow drips over it on the glacier walls below were great splotches, for all the world as though a gigantic ink-pot had been upset.

Second camp in the Grand Basin—looking down, 16,500 feet.

The Flagstaff

While we sat resting awhile on our way to this camp, gazing at these pinnacles of the North Peak, we fell to talking about the pioneer climbers of this mountain who claimed to have set a flagstaff near the summit of the North Peak—as to which feat a great deal of incredulity existed in Alaska for several reasons—and we renewed our determination that, if the weather permitted when we had reached our goal and ascended the South Peak, we would climb the North Peak also to seek for traces of this earliest exploit on Denali, which is dealt with at length in another place in this book. All at once Walter cried out: "I see the flagstaff!" Eagerly pointing to the rocky prominence nearest the summit—the summit itself is covered with snow—he added: "I see it plainly!" Karstens, looking where he pointed, saw it also, and, whipping out the field-glasses, one by one we all looked, and saw it distinctly standing out against the sky. With the naked eye I was never able to see it unmistakably, but through the glasses it stood out, sturdy and strong, one side covered with crusted snow. We were greatly rejoiced that we could carry down positive confirmation of this matter. It was no longer necessary for us to ascend the North Peak.

The upper glacier also bore plain signs of the

earthquake that had shattered the ridge. Huge blocks of ice were strewn upon it, ripped off the left-hand wall, but it was nowhere crevassed as badly as the lower glacier, but much more broken up into sérac. Some of the bergs presented very beautiful sights, wind-carved incrustations of snow in cameo upon their blue surface giving a suggestion of Wedgwood pottery. All tints seemed more delicate and beautiful up here than on the lower glacier.

On the 5th June we advanced to about seventeen thousand five hundred feet right up the middle of the glacier. As we rose that morning slowly out of the flat in which our tent was pitched and began to climb the steep sérac, clouds that had been gathering below swept rapidly up into the Grand Basin, and others swept as rapidly over the summits and down upon us. In a few moments we were in a dense smother of vapor with nothing visible a couple of hundred yards away. Then the temperature dropped, and soon snow was falling which increased to a heavy snow-storm that raged an hour. We made our camp and ate our lunch, and by that time the smother of vapor passed, the sun came out hot again, and we were all simultaneously overtaken with a deep drowsiness and slept. Then out into the glare again, to

Third camp in the Grand Basin—17,000 feet, showing the shattering of the glacier walls by the earthquake.

The rocks at the top of the picture are about 19,000 feet high and are the highest rocks on the south peak of the mountain.

go down and bring up the remainder of the stuff, we went, and that night we were established in our last camp but one. We had decided to go up at least five hundred feet farther that we might have the less to climb when we made our final attack upon the peak. So when we returned with the loads from below we did not stop at camp, but carried them forward and cached them against to-morrow's final move.

On Friday, the 6th June, we made our last move and pitched our tent in a flat near the base of the ridge, just below the final rise in the glacier of the Grand Basin, at about eighteen thousand feet, and we were able to congratulate one another on making the highest camp ever made in North America. I set up and read the mercurial barometer, and when corrected for its own temperature it stood at 15.061. The boiling-point thermometer registered 180.5, as the point at which water boiled, with an air temperature of 35°. It took one hour to boil the rice for supper. The aneroids stood at 14.8 and 14.9, still steadily losing on the mercurial barometer. I think that a rough altitude gauge could be calculated from the time rice takes to boil—at least as reliable as an aneroid barometer. At the Parker Pass it took fifty minutes; here it took sixty. This is about the height of perpetual snow on the great Himalayan peaks; but we had been above the perpetual snow-line for forty-eight days.

We were now within about two thousand five hundred feet of the summit and had two weeks' full supply of food and fuel, which, at a pinch, could be stretched to three weeks. Certain things were short: the chocolate and figs and raisins and salt were low; of the zwieback there remained but two and one-half packages, reserved against lunch when we attacked the summit. But the meat-balls, the erbswurst, the caribou jelly, the rice, and the tea—our staples—were abundant for two weeks, with four gallons of coal-oil and a gallon of alcohol. The end of our painful transportation hither was accomplished; we were within one day's climb of the summit with supplies to besiege. If the weather should prove persistently bad we could wait; we could advance our parallels; could put another camp on the ridge itself at nineteen thousand feet, and yet another half-way up the dome. If we had to fight our way step by step and could advance but a couple of hundred feet a day, we were still confident that, barring unforeseeable misfortunes, we could reach the top. But we wanted a clear day on top, that the observations we designed to make could be made; it

The North Peak, 20,000 feet high.

Our last camp in the Grand Basin, at 18,000 feet: the highest camp ever made in North America.

would be a poor success that did but set our feet on the highest point. And we felt sure that, prepared as we were to wait, the clear day would come.

As so often happens when everything unpropitious is guarded against, nothing unpropitious occurs. It would have been a wonderful chance, indeed, if, supplied only for one day, a fine, clear day had come. But supplied against bad weather for two or three weeks, it was no wonder at all that the very first day should have presented itself bright and clear. We had exhausted our bad fortune below; here, at the juncture above all others at which we should have chosen to enjoy it, we were to encounter our good fortune.

But here, where all signs seemed to promise success to the expedition, the author began to have fears of personal failure. The story of Mr. Fitzgerald's expedition to Aconcagua came to his mind, and he recalled that, although every other member of the party reached the summit, that gentleman himself was unable to do so. In the last stage the difficulty of breathing had increased with fits of smothering, and the medicine chest held no remedy for blind staggers.

CHAPTER V

THE ULTIMATE HEIGHT

WE lay down for a few hours on the night of the 6th June, resolved to rise at three in the morning for our attempt upon the summit of Denali. At supper Walter had made a desperate effort to use some of our ten pounds of flour in the manufacture of "noodles" with which to thicken the stew. We had continued to pack that flour and had made effort after effort to cook it in some eatable way, but without success. The sour dough would not ferment, and we had no baking-powder. *Is* there any way to cook flour under such circumstances? But he made the noodles too large and did not cook them enough, and they wrought internal havoc upon those who partook of them. Three of the four of us were unwell all night. The digestion is certainly more delicate and more easily disturbed at great altitudes than at the lower levels. While Karstens and Tatum were tossing uneasily in the bedclothes, the writer sat up with a blanket round his shoulders, crouching over the primus stove, with the thermometer at −21° F. outdoors. Walter alone was at ease, with digestive and somnolent capabilities proof against any invasion. It was, of course, broad daylight all night. At three the company was aroused, and, after partaking of a very light breakfast indeed, we sallied forth into the brilliant, clear morning with not a cloud in the sky. The only packs we carried that day were the instruments and the lunch. The sun was shining, but a keen north wind was blowing and the thermometer stood at −4° F. We were rather a sorry company. Karstens still had internal pains; Tatum and I had severe headaches. Walter was the only one feeling entirely himself, so Walter was put in the lead and in the lead he remained all day.

We took a straight course up the great snow ridge directly south of our camp and then around the peak into which it rises; quickly told but slowly and most laboriously done. It was necessary to make the traverse high up on this peak instead of around its base, so much had its ice and snow been shattered by the earthquake on the lower portions. Once around this peak, there rose before us the horseshoe ridge which carries the ultimate height of Denali, a horseshoe ridge of snow opening to the east with a low snow peak at either end, the centre of the ridge soaring above both peaks. Above us was nothing visible but snow; the rocks were all beneath, the last rocks standing at about 19,000 feet. Our progress was exceedingly slow. It was bitterly cold; all the morning toes and fingers were without sensation, kick them and beat them as we would. We were all clad in full winter hand and foot gear—more gear than had sufficed at 50° below zero on the Yukon trail. Within the writer's No. 16 moccasins were three pairs of heavy hand-knitted woollen socks, two pairs of camel's-hair socks, and a pair of thick felt socks; while underneath them, between them and the iron "creepers," were the soles cut from a pair of felt shoes. Upon his hands were a pair of the thickest Scotch wool gloves, thrust inside huge lynx-paw mitts lined with Hudson Bay duffle. His moose-hide breeches and shirt, worn all the winter on the trail, were worn throughout this climb; over the shirt was a thick sweater and over all the usual Alaskan "parkee" amply furred around the hood; underneath was a suit of the heaviest Jaeger underwear—yet until nigh noon feet were like lumps of iron and fingers were constantly numb. That north wind was cruelly cold, and there can be

The South Peak from about 18,000 feet.

The ridge with two peaks in the background is shaped like a horseshoe, and the highest point on the mountain is on another little ridge just beyond, parallel with the ridge that shows, almost at the middle point between the two peaks.

no possible question that cold is felt much more keenly in the thin air of nineteen thousand feet than it is below. But the north wind was really our friend, for nothing but a north wind will drive all vapor from this mountain. Karstens beat his feet so violently and so continually against the hard snow to restore the circulation that two of his toe-nails sloughed off afterward. By eleven o'clock we had been climbing for six hours and were well around the peak, advancing toward the horseshoe ridge, but even then there were grave doubts if we should succeed in reaching it that day, it was so cold. A hint from any member of the party that his feet were actually freezing—a hint expected all along—would have sent us all back. When there is no sensation left in the feet at all it is, however, difficult to be quite sure if they be actually freezing or not—and each one was willing to give the attempt upon the summit the benefit of the doubt. What should we have done with the ordinary leather climbing boots? But once entirely around the peak we were in a measure sheltered from the north wind, and the sun full upon us gave more warmth. It was hereabouts, and not, surely, at the point indicated in the photograph in Mr. Belmore Browne's book, that the climbing party of last year was driven back by the blizzard that descended upon them when close to their goal. Not until we had stopped for lunch and had drunk the scalding tea from the thermos bottles, did we all begin to have confidence that this day would see the completion of the ascent. But the writer's shortness of breath became more and more distressing as he rose. The familiar fits of panting took a more acute form; at such times everything would turn black before his eyes and he would choke and gasp and seem unable to get breath at all. Yet a few moments' rest restored him completely, to struggle on another twenty or thirty paces and to sink gasping upon the snow again. All were more affected in the breathing than they had been at any time before—it was curious to see every man's mouth open for breathing—but none of the others in this distressing way. Before the traverse around the peak just mentioned, Walter had noticed the writer's growing discomfort and had insisted upon assuming the mercurial barometer. The boy's eager kindness was gladly accepted and the instrument was surrendered. So it did not fall to the writer's credit to carry the thing to the top as he had wished.

The climbing grew steeper and steeper; the slope that had looked easy from below now seemed to shoot straight up. For the most part the climbing-irons gave us sufficient footing, but here and there we came to softer snow, where they would not take sufficient hold and we had to cut steps. The calks in these climbing-irons were about an inch and a quarter long; we wished they had been two inches. The creepers are a great advantage in the matter of speed, but they need long points. They are not so safe as step-cutting, and there is the ever-present danger that unless one is exceedingly careful one will step upon the rope with them and their sharp calks sever some of the strands. They were, however, of great assistance and saved a deal of laborious step-cutting.

At last the crest of the ridge was reached and we stood well above the two peaks that mark the ends of the horseshoe.*

Also it was evident that we were well above the great North Peak across the Grand Basin.

*The dotted line on the photograph opposite page 346 of Mr. Belmore Browne's book, "The Conquest of Mt. McKinley," does not, in the writer's opinion, represent the real course taken by Professor Parker, Mr. Belmore Browne, and Merl Le Voy in their approach to the summit, and it is easy to understand the confusion of direction in the fierce storm that descended upon the party. If, as the dots show, the party went to the summit of the right-hand peak, they went out of their way and had still a considerable distance to travel. "Perhaps five minutes of easy walking would have taken us to the highest point," says Mr. Browne. It is probably more than

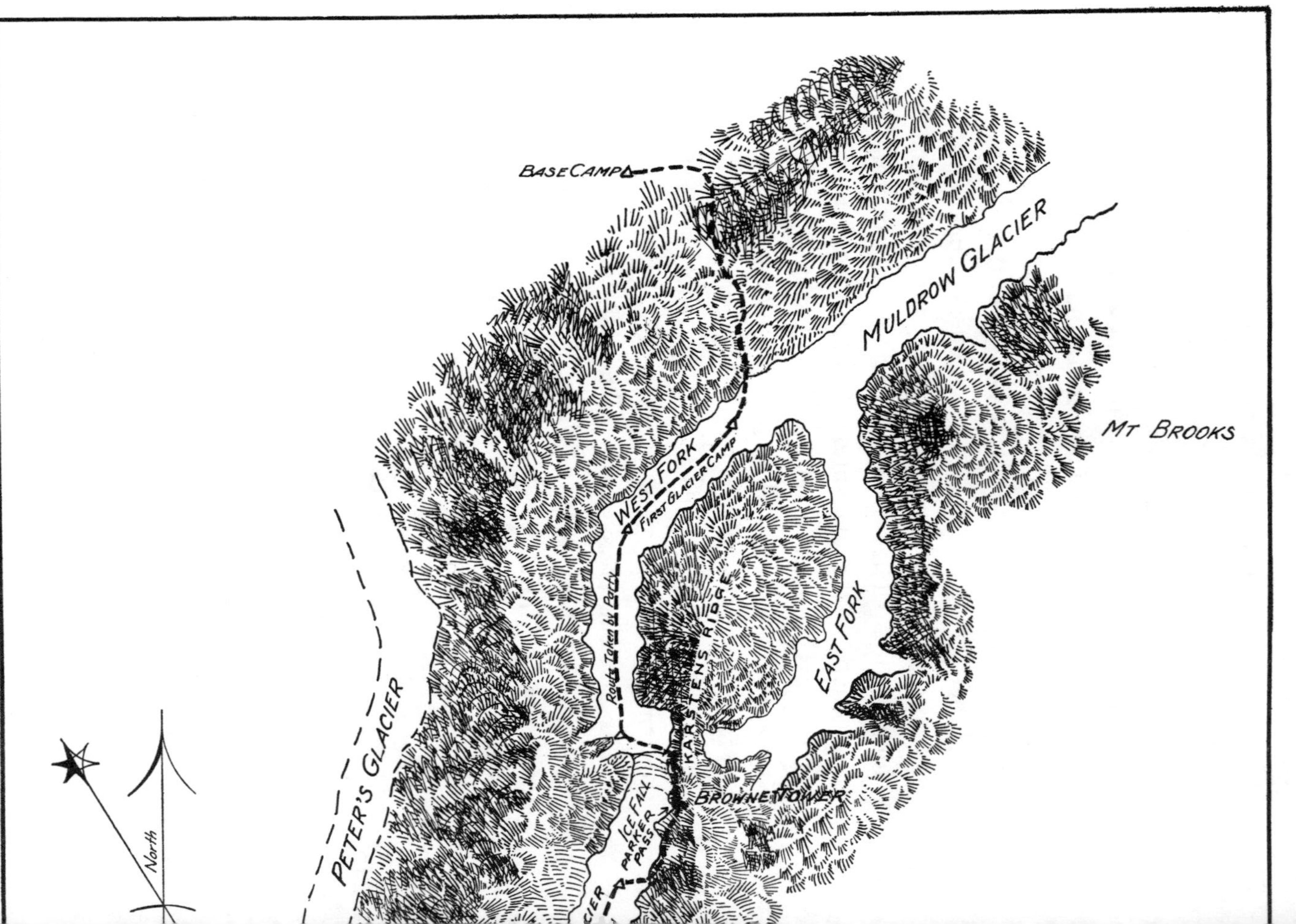

Base Camp
Muldrow Glacier
Mt Brooks
West Fork
First Glacier Camp
Route Taken by Party
Karstens Ridge
East Fork
Browne Tower
Ice Fall
Parker Pass
Peter's Glacier
North

MT DENALI (MCKINLEY)
Elevation 20,700 ft. above S.L.

MAP SHOWING
ROUTE OF THE STUCK-KARSTENS
EXPEDITION TO THE SUMMIT OF
MT. DENALI (MT. MCKINLEY.)
1913

0 1 2 3 4 5
APPROXIMATE SCALE OF MILES

NB. This map is based on sketches and compass observations made by members of the Stuck-Karstens party, and is only approximately correct.

DENALI'S WIFE
(MT. FORAKER.)

Its crest had been like an index on the snow beside us as we climbed, and we stopped for a few moments when it seemed that we were level with it. We judged it to be about five hundred feet lower than the South Peak.

But still there stretched ahead of us, and perhaps one hundred feet above us, another small ridge with a north and south pair of little haycock summits. This is the real top of Denali. From below, this ultimate ridge merges indistinguishably with the crest of the horseshoe ridge, but it is not a part of it but a culminating ridge beyond it. With keen excitement we pushed on. Walter, who had been in the lead all day, was the first to scramble up; a native Alaskan, he is the first human being to set foot upon the top of Alaska's great mountain, and he had well earned the lifelong distinction. Karstens and Tatum were hard upon his heels, but the last man on the

a mile from the summit of the snow peak shown in the picture to the actual summit of the mountain. One who took that course would have to descend from the peak and then ascend the horseshoe ridge, and the highest point of the horseshoe ridge is perhaps two hundred feet above the summit of this snow peak. In the opinion that Professor Parker expressed to the writer, the dotted lines should bear much more to the left, making directly for the centre of the horseshoe ridge, which is the obvious course. But it should again be said that men in the circumstances and condition of this party when forced to turn back, may be pardoned for mistaking the exact direction in which they had been proceeding.

The climbing-irons.

rope, in his enthusiasm and excitement somewhat overpassing his narrow wind margin, had almost to be hauled up the last few feet, and fell unconscious for a moment upon the floor of the little snow basin that occupies the top of the mountain. This, then, is the actual summit, a little crater-like snow basin, sixty or sixty-five feet long and twenty to twenty-five feet wide, with a haycock of snow at either end—the south one a little higher than the north. On the southwest this little basin is much corniced, and the whole thing looked as though every severe storm might somewhat change its shape.

So soon as wind was recovered we shook hands all round and a brief prayer of thanksgiving to Almighty God was said, that He had granted us our hearts' desire and brought us safely to the top of His great mountain.

This prime duty done, we fell at once to our scientific tasks. The instrument-tent was set up, the mercurial barometer, taken out of its leather case and then out of its wooden case, was swung upon its tripod and a rough zero established, and it was left awhile to adjust itself to conditions before a reading was attempted. It was a great gratification to get it to the top uninjured. The boiling-point apparatus was put together and its candle lighted under the ice which filled its little cistern. The three-inch, three-circle aneroid was read at once at thirteen and two-tenths inches, its mendacious altitude scale confidently pointing at twenty-three thousand three hundred feet. Half an hour later it had dropped to 13.175 inches and had shot us up another one hundred feet into the air. Soon the water was boiling in the little tubes of the boiling-point thermometer and the steam pouring out of the vent. The thread of mercury rose to 174.9° and stayed there. There is something definite and uncompromising about the boiling-point hypsometer; no tapping will make it rise or fall; it reaches its mark unmistakably and does not budge. The reading of the mercurial barometer is a slower and more delicate business. It takes a good light and a good sight to tell when the ivory zero-point is exactly touching the surface of the mercury in the cistern; it takes care and precision to get the vernier exactly level with the top of the column. It was read, some half-hour after it was set up, at 13.617 inches. The alcohol minimum thermometer stood at 7° F. all the while we were on top. Meanwhile, Tatum had been reading a round of angles with the prismatic compass. He could not handle it with sufficient exactness with his mitts on, and he froze his fingers doing it bare-handed.

The scientific work accomplished, then and not till then did we indulge ourselves in the wonderful prospect that stretched around us. It was a perfectly clear day, the sun shining brightly in the sky, and naught bounded our view save the natural limitations of vision. Immediately before us, in the direction in which we had climbed, lay —nothing: a void, a sheer gulf many thousands of feet deep, and one shrank back instinctively from the little parapet of the snow basin when one had glanced at the awful profundity. Across the gulf, about three thousand feet beneath us and fifteen or twenty miles away, sprang most splendidly into view the great mass of Denali's Wife, or Mount Foraker, as some white men misname her, filling majestically all the middle distance. It was our first glimpse of her during the whole ascent. Denali's Wife does not appear at all save from the actual summit of Denali, for she is completely hidden by his South Peak until the moment when his South Peak is surmounted. And never was nobler sight displayed to man than that great, isolated mountain spread out completely, with all its spurs and ridges, its cliffs and its glaciers, lofty and mighty and yet far beneath us. On that spot one understood why the view of Denali from Lake Minchúmina is the grand view, for the west face drops abruptly down with nothing but that vast void from the top to nigh the bottom of the mountain. Beyond stretched, blue and vague to the southwest, the wide valley of the Kuskokwim, with an end of all mountains. To the north we looked right over the North Peak to the foot-hills below, patched with lakes and lingering snow, glittering with streams. We had hoped to see the junction of the Yukon and Tanana Rivers, one hundred and fifty miles away to the northwest, as we had often and often seen the summit of Denali from that point in the winter, but the haze that almost always qualifies a fine summer day inhibited that stretch of vision. Perhaps the forest-fires we found raging on the Tanana River were already beginning to foul the northern sky.

It was, however, to the south and the east that the most marvellous prospect opened before us. What infinite tangle of mountain ranges filled the whole scene, until gray sky, gray mountain, and gray sea merged in the ultimate distance! The near-by peaks and ridges stood out with dazzling distinction, the glaciation, the drainage, the relation of each part to the others all revealed. The

Denali's Wife from the summit of Denali

snow-covered tops of the remoter peaks, dwindling and fading, rose to our view as though floating in thin air when their bases were hidden by the haze, and the beautiful crescent curve of the whole Alaskan range exhibited itself from Denali to the sea. To the right hand the glittering, tiny threads of streams draining the mountain range into the Chulitna and Sushitna Rivers, and so to Cook's Inlet and the Pacific Ocean, spread themselves out; to the left the affluents of the Kantishna and the Nenana drained the range into the Yukon and Bering Sea.

Yet the chief impression was not of our connection with the earth so far below, its rivers and its seas, but rather of detachment from it. We seemed alone upon a dead world, as dead as the mountains on the moon. Only once before can the writer remember a similar feeling of being neither in the world or of the world, and that was at the bottom of the Grand Cañon of the Colorado, in Arizona, its savage granite walls as dead as this savage peak of ice.

Above us the sky took a blue so deep that none of us had ever gazed upon a midday sky like it before. It was a deep, rich, lustrous, transparent blue, as dark as a Prussian blue, but intensely blue; a hue so strange, so increasingly impressive, that to one at least it "seemed like special news of God," as a new poet sings. We first noticed the darkening tint of the upper sky in the Grand Basin, and it deepened as we rose. Tyndall observed and discussed this phenomenon in the Alps, but it seems scarcely to have been mentioned since.

It is difficult to describe at all the scene which the top of the mountain presented, and impossible to describe it adequately. One was not occupied with the thought of description but wholly possessed with the breadth and glory of it, with its sheer, amazing immensity and scope. Only once, perhaps, in any lifetime is such vision granted, certainly never before had been vouchsafed to any of us. Not often in the summertime does Denali completely unveil himself and dismiss the clouds from all the earth beneath. Yet we could not linger, unique though the occasion, dearly bought our privilege; the miserable limitations of the flesh gave us continual warning to depart; we grew colder and still more wretchedly cold. The thermometer stood at 7° in the full sunshine, and the north wind was keener than ever. My fingers were so cold that I would not venture to withdraw them from the mittens to change the film in the camera, and the other men

Robert Tatum raising the Stars and Stripes on the highest point in North America.

This photograph was exposed upon a previous exposure.

were in like case; indeed, our hands were by this time so numb as to make it almost impossible to operate a camera at all. A number of photographs had been taken, though not half we should have liked to take, but it is probable that, however many more exposures had been made, they would have been little better than those we got. Our top-of-the-mountain photography was a great disappointment. One thing we learned: exposures at such altitude should be longer than those below, perhaps owing to the darkness of the sky.

When the mercurial barometer had been read the tent was thrown down and abandoned, the first of the series of abandonments that marked our descent from the mountain. The tent-pole was used for a moment as a flagstaff while Tatum hoisted a little United States flag he had patiently and skilfully constructed in our camps below out of two silk handkerchiefs and the cover of a sewing-bag. Then the pole was put to its permanent use. It had already been carved with a suitable inscription, and now a transverse piece, already prepared and fitted, was lashed securely to it and it was planted on one of the little snow turrets of the summit—the sign of our redemption, high above North America. Only some peaks in the Andes and some peaks in the Himalayas rise above it in all the world. It was of light, dry birch and, though six feet in length, so slender that we think it may weather many a gale. And Walter thrust it into the snow so firmly at a blow that it could not be withdrawn again. Then we gathered about it and said the Te Deum.

It was 1.30 P. M. when we reached the summit and two minutes past three when we left; yet so quickly had the time flown that we could not believe we had been an hour and a half on top. The journey down was a long, weary grind, the longer and the wearier that we made a dĕtour and went out of our way to seek for Professor Parker's thermometer, which he had left "in a crack on the west side of the last boulder of the north-east ridge." That sounds definite enough, yet in fact it is equivocal. "Which is the last boulder?" we disputed as we went down the slope. A long series of rocks almost in line came to an end, with one rock a little below the others, a little out of the line. This egregious boulder would, it seemed to me, naturally be called the last; Karstens thought not—thought the "last boulder" was the last *on* the ridge. As we learned later, Karstens was right, and since he yielded to me we did not find the thermometer, for, having descended to this isolated rock, we would not climb up again

The saying of the Te Deum.

This picture was snapped three times instead of once. Karstens' fingers were freezing and the bulb-release was broken. Only three figures were in the group.

for fifty thermometers. One's disappointment is qualified by the knowledge that the thermometer is probably not of adequate scale, Professor Parker's recollection being that it read only to 60° below zero, F. A lower temperature than this is recorded every winter on the Yukon River.

A thermometer reading to 100° below zero, left at this spot, would, in my judgment, perhaps yield a lower minimum than has ever yet been authentically recorded on earth, and it is most unfortunate that the opportunity was lost. Yet I did not leave my own alcohol minimum—scaled to 95° below zero, and yielding, by estimation, perhaps ten degrees below the scaling—there, because of the difficulty of giving explicit directions that should lead to its ready recovery, and at the close of such a day of toil as is involved in reaching the summit, men have no stomach for prolonged search. As will be told, it is cached lower down, but at a spot where it cannot be missed.

However, for one, the writer was largely unconscious of weariness in that descent. All the way down, my thoughts were occupied with the glorious scene my eyes had gazed upon and should gaze upon never again. In all human probability I would never climb that mountain again; yet if I climbed it a score more times I would never be likely to repeat such vision. Commonly, only for a few hours at a time, never for more than a few days at a time, save in the dead of winter when climbing is out of the question, does Denali completely unveil himself and dismiss the clouds from all the earth beneath him. Not for long, with these lofty colds contiguous, will the vapors of Cook's Inlet and Prince William Sound and the whole North Pacific Ocean refrain from sweeping upward; their natural trend is hitherward. As the needle turns to the magnet so the clouds find an irresistible attraction in this great mountain mass, and though the inner side of the range be rid of them the sea side is commonly filled to overflowing.

Only those who have for long years cherished a great and almost inordinate desire, and have had that desire gratified to the limit of their expectation, can enter into the deep thankfulness and content that filled the heart upon the descent of this mountain. There was no pride of conquest, no trace of that exultation of victory some enjoy upon the first ascent of a lofty peak, no gloating over good fortune that had hoisted us a few hundred feet higher than others who had struggled and been discomfited. Rather was the feeling that a privileged communion with the high places of the earth had been granted; that not only had we been permitted to lift up eager eyes to these summits, secret and solitary since the world began, but to enter boldly upon them, to take place, as it were, domestically in their hitherto sealed chambers, to inhabit them, and to cast our eyes down from them, seeing all things as they spread out from the windows of heaven itself.

Into this strong yet serene emotion, into this reverent elevation of spirit, came with a shock a recollection of some recent reading.

Oh, wisdom of man and the apparatus of the sciences, the little columns of mercury that sling up and down, the vacuum boxes that expand and contract, the hammer that chips the highest rocks, the compass that takes the bearings of glacier and ridge—all the equipage of hypsometry and geology and geodesy—how pitifully feeble and childish it seems to cope with the majesty of the mountains! Take them all together, haul them up the steep, and as they lie there, read, recorded, and done for, which shall be more adequate to the whole scene—their records?—or that simple, ancient hymn, "We praise Thee, O God! —Heaven and earth are full of the majesty of Thy Glory!" What an astonishing thing that, standing where we stood and seeing what we saw, there are men who should be able to deduce this law or that from their observation of its working and yet be unable to see the Lawgiver!—who should be able to push back effect to immediate cause and yet be blind to the Supreme Cause of All Causes; who can say, "This is the glacier's doing and it is marvellous in our eyes," and not see Him "Who in His Strength setteth fast the mountains and is girded with power," Whose servants the glaciers, the snow, and the ice are, "wind and storm fulfilling His Word"; who exult in the exercise of their own intelligences and the playthings those intelligences have constructed and yet deny the Omniscience that endowed them with some minute fragment of Itself! It was not always so; it was not so with the really great men who have advanced our knowledge of nature. But of late years hordes of small men have given themselves up to the study of the physical sciences without any study preliminary. It would almost seem nowadays that whoever can sit in the seat of the scornful may sit in the seat of learning.

A good many years ago, on an occasion already referred to, the writer roamed through the depths of the Grand Cañon with a chance acquaintance who described himself as "Herpetologist to the Academy of Sciences" in some Western or Mid-Western State, and as this gentleman found the curious little reptiles he was in search of under a root or in a cranny of rock he repeated their many-syllabled names. Curious to know what these names literally meant and whence derived, the writer made inquiry, sometimes hazarding a conjectural etymology. To his astonishment and dismay he found this "scientist," whom he had looked up to, entirely ignorant of the meaning of the terms he employed. They were just arbitrary terms to him. The little hopping and crawling creatures might as well have been numbered, or called x, y, z, for any significance their formidable nomenclature held for him. Yet this man had been keenly sarcastic about the Noachian deluge and had jeered from the height of his superiority at hoary records which he knew only at second-hand reference, and had laid it down that if the human race became extinct the birds would stand the best chance of "evolving a primate"! Since that time other "scientists" have been encountered, with no better equipment, with no history, no poetry, no philosophy in any broad sense, men with no letters—illiterate, strictly speaking—yet with all the dogmatism in the world. Can any one be more dogmatic than your modern scientist? The reproach has passed altogether to him from the theologian.

The thing grows, and its menace and scandal grow with it. Since coming "outside" the writer has encountered a professor at a college, a Ph.D. of a great university, who confessed that he had never heard of certain immortal characters of Dickens whose names are household words. We shall have to open Night-Schools for Scientists, where men who have been deprived of all early advantages may learn the rudiments of English literature. One wishes that Dickens himself might have dealt with their pretensions, but they are since his day. And surely it is time some one started a movement for suppressing illiterate Ph.D.'s.

Of this class, one feels sure, are the scientific heroes of the sensational articles in the monthly magazines of the baser sort, of which we picked up a number in the Kantishna on our way to the mountain. Here, in a picture that seems to have obtruded itself bodily into a page of letter-press, or else to have suffered the accidental irruption of a page of letter-press all around it, you shall see a grave scientist looking anxiously down a very large microscope, and shall read that he has transferred a kidney from a cat to a dog, and therefore we can no longer believe in the immortality of the soul; or else that he has succeeded in artificially fertilizing the ova of a starfish—or was it a jellyfish?—and therefore there is no God; not just in so many bald words, of course, but in unmistakable import. Or it may be—so commonly does the crassest credulity go hand in hand with the blankest scepticism—he has discovered the germ of old age and is hot upon the track of another germ that shall destroy it, so that we may all live virtually as long as we like; which, of course, disposes once for all of a world to come. The Psalmist was not always complaisant or even temperate in his language, but he lived a long time ago and must be pardoned; his curt summary stands: "Dixit insipiens!" But the writer vows that if he were addicted to the pursuit of any branch of physical knowledge he would insist upon being called by the name of that branch. He would be a physiologist or a biologist or an anatomist or even a herpetologist, but none should call him "scientist." As Doll Tearsheet says in the second part of "King Henry IV": "These villains will make the word as odious as the word 'occupy'; which was an excellent good word before it was ill-sorted." If Doctor Johnson were compiling an English dictionary to-day he would define "scientist" something thus: "A cant name for an experimenter in some department of physical knowledge, commonly furnished with arrogance and dogmatism, but devoid of real learning."

Here is no gibe at the physical sciences. To sneer at them were just as foolish as to sneer at religion. What we could do on this expedition in a "scientific" way we did laboriously and zealously. We would never have thought of attempting the ascent of the mountain without bringing back whatever little addition to human knowledge was within the scope of our powers and opportunities. Tatum took rounds of angles, in practice against the good fortune of a clear day on top, on every possible occasion. The sole personal credit the present writer takes concerning the whole enterprise is the packing of that mercurial barometer on his back, from the Tanana River nearly to the top of the mountain, a point at which he was compelled to relinquish it to another. He has always had his opinion about mountain climbers who put an aneroid in their pocket and go to the top of a great, new peak and come down confidently announcing its height. But when all this business is done as closely and carefully as possible, and every observation taken that there are instruments devised to record, surely the soul is dead that feels no more and sees no further than the instruments do, that stirs with no other emotion than the mercury in the tube or the dial at its point of suspension, that is incapable of awe, of reverence, of worshipful uplift, and does not feel that "the Lord even the most mighty God hath spoken, and called the world from the rising of the sun even to the going down of the same," in the wonders displayed before his eyes.

We reached our eighteen-thousand-foot camp about five o'clock, a weary but happy crew. It was written in the diary that night: "I remember no day in my life so full of toil, distress, and exhaustion, and yet so full of happiness and keen gratification."

The culminating day should not be allowed to pass without another tribute to the efficiency of the amber glasses. Notwithstanding the glare of the sun at twenty thousand feet and upward, no one had the slightest irritation of the eyes. There has never been an April of travel on the Yukon in eight years that the writer has not suffered from inflammation of the eyes despite the darkest smoke-colored glasses that could be procured. A naked candle at a road-house would give a stab of pain every time the eyes encountered it, and reading would become almost impossible. The amber glasses, however, while leaving vision almost as bright as without them, filter out the rays that cause the irritation and afford perfect protection against the consequences of sun and glare. There is only one improvement to make in the amber glasses, and that is some device of air-tight cells that shall prevent them from fogging when the cold on the outside of the glass condenses the moisture of perspiration on the inside of the glass. We use double-glazed sashes with an air space between on all windows in our houses in Alaska and find ourselves no longer incommoded by frost on the panes; some adaptation of this principle should be within the skill of the optician and would remove a very troublesome defect in all snow-glasses.

If some one would invent a preventive against shortness of breath as efficient as amber glasses are against snow-blindness, climbing at great altitudes would lose all its terrors for one mountaineer. So far as it was possible to judge, no other member of the party was near his altitude limit. There seemed no reason why Karstens and Walter in particular should not go another ten thousand feet, were there a mountain in the world ten thousand feet higher than Denali, but the writer knows that he himself could not have gone much higher.

CHAPTER VI

THE RETURN

THE next day was another bright, cloudless day, the second and last of them. Perhaps never did men abandon as cheerfully stuff that had been freighted as laboriously as we abandoned our surplus baggage at the eighteen-thousand-foot camp. We made a great pile of it in the lee of one of the ice-blocks of the glacier—food, coal-oil, clothing, and bedding—covering all with the wolf-robe and setting up a shovel as a mark; though just why we cached it so carefully, or for whom, no one of us would be able to say. It will probably be a long time ere any others camp in that Grand Basin. While yet such a peak is unclimbed, there is constant goading of mountaineering minds to its conquest; once its top has been reached, the incentive declines. Much exploring work is yet to do on Denali; the day will doubtless come when all its peaks and ridges and glaciers will be duly mapped, but our view from the summit agreed with our study of its conformation during the ascent, that no other route will be found to the top. When first we were cutting and climbing on the ridge, and had glimpses, as the mists cleared, of the glacier on the other side and the ridges that arose from it, we thought that perhaps they might afford a passage, but from above the appearance changed and seemed to forbid it altogether. At times, almost in despair at the task which the Northeast Ridge presented, we would look across at the ice-covered rocks of the North Peak and dream that they might be climbed, but they are really quite impossible. The south side has been tried again and again and no approach discovered, nor did it appear from the top that such approach exists; the west side is sheer precipice; the north side is covered with a great hanging glacier and is devoid of practicable slopes; it has been twice attempted. Only on the northeast has the glacier cut so deeply into the mountain as to give access to the heights.

June 8th was Sunday, but we had to take advantage of the clear, bright day to get as far down the mountain as possible. The stuff it was still necessary to pack made good, heavy loads, and we knew not what had happened to our staircase in our absence.

Having said Morning Prayer, we left at 9.30 A. M., after a night in which all of us slept soundly—the first sound sleep some had enjoyed for a long time. Contentment and satisfaction are great somnifacients. The Grand Basin was glorious in sunshine, the peaks crystal-clear against a cloudless sky, the huge blocks of ice thrown down by the earthquake and scattered all over the glacier gleamed white in the sunshine, deep-blue in the shadow. We wound our way downward, passing camp site after camp site, until at the first place we camped in the Grand Basin we stopped for lunch. Then we made the traverse under the cliffs to the Parker Pass, which we reached at 1.30 P. M. The sun was hot; there was not a breath of wind; we were exceedingly thirsty and we decided to light the primus stove and make a big pot of tea and replenish the thermos bottles before attempting the descent of the ridge. While this was doing a place was found to cache the minimum thermometer and a tin can that had held a photographic film, in which we had placed a record of our ascent. Above, we had not found any distinctive place in which a record could be deposited with the assurance that it would be found by any one seeking it. One feels sure that in the depth of winter very great cold must occur even at this elevation. Yet we should have liked to leave it much higher. Without some means, which we did not possess, of marking a position, there would, however, have been little use in leaving it amid the boulders where we hunted unsuccessfully for Professor Parker's instrument. We had hoped to be able to grave some sign upon the rocks with the geological hammer, but the first time it was brought down upon the granite its point splintered in the same exasperating way that the New York dealer's fancy ice-axes behaved when it was attempted to put them to practical use. "Warranted cast steel" upon an implement ought to be a warning not to purchase it for mountain work. Tool-steel alone will serve.

Our little record cache at the Parker Pass, placed at the foot of the west or upward-facing side of the great slab which marks the natural camping site, should stand there for many years. It is not a place where snow lies deep or long, and it will surely be found by any who seek it. We took our last looks up into the Grand Basin, still brilliant in the sunshine, our last looks at the summit, still cloudless and clear. There was a melancholy even in the midst of triumph in looking for the last time at these scenes where we had so greatly hoped and endeavored—and had been so amply rewarded. We recalled the eager expectation with which we first gazed up between these granite slabs into the long-hidden basin, a week before, and there was sadness in the feeling that in all probability we should never have this noble view again.

Before the reader turns his back upon the Grand Basin once for all, I should like to put a name upon the glacier it contains—since it is the fashion to name glaciers. I should like to call it the Harper Glacier, after my half-breed companion of three years, who was the first human being to reach the summit of the mountain. This reason might suffice, but there is another and most interesting reason for associating the name Harper with this mountain. Arthur Harper, Walter's father, the pioneer of all Alaskan miners, "the first man who thought of trying the Yukon as a mining field so far as we know," as William Ogilvie tells us in his "Early Days on the Yukon" * (and none had better opportunity of knowing than Ogilvie), was also the first man to make written reference to this mountain, since Vancouver, the great navigator, saw it from the head of Cook's Inlet in 1794.

* Ottawa: Thorburn & Abbott, 1913, p. 87.

Arthur Harper, in company with Al. Mayo, made the earliest exploration of the Tanana River, ascending that stream in the summer of 1878 to about the present site of Fairbanks; and in a letter to E. W. Nelson, of the United States Biological Survey, then on the Alaskan coast, Harper wrote the following winter of the "great ice mountain to the south" as one of the most wonderful sights of the trip.* It is pleasant to think that a son of his, yet unborn, was to be the first to set foot on its top; pleasantly also the office of setting his name upon the lofty glacier, the gleam from which caught his eye and roused his wonder thirty years ago, falls upon one who has been glad and proud to take, in some measure, his place.

Then began the difficulty and the danger, the toil and the anxiety, of the descent of the ridge. Karstens led, then followed Tatum, then the writer, and then Walter. The unbroken surface of the ridge above the cleavage is sensationally steep, and during our absence nearly two feet of new snow had fallen upon it. The steps that had been shovelled as we ascended were entirely obliterated and it was necessary to shovel new ones; it was the very heat of the day, and by the can-

* "Mt. McKinley Region": Alfred H. Brooks, Washington, 1911, p. 25.

Beginning the descent of the ridge; looking down 4,000 feet upon the Muldrow Glacier.

ons of climbing we should have camped at the Pass and descended in the early morning. But all were eager to get down, and we ventured it. Now that our task was accomplished, our minds reverted to the boy at the base camp long anxiously expecting us, and we thought of him and spoke of him continually and speculated how he had fared. One feels upon reflection that we took more risk in descending that ridge than we took at any time in the ascent. But Karstens was most cautious and careful, and in the long and intensive apprenticeship of this expedition had become most expert. I sometimes wondered whether Swiss guides would have much to teach either him or Walter in snow-craft; their chief instruction would probably be along the line of taking more chances, wisely. If the writer had to ascend this mountain again he would intrust himself to Karstens and Walter rather than to any Swiss guides he has known, for ice and snow in Alaska are not quite the same as ice and snow in the Alps or the Canadian Rockies.

The loose snow was shovelled away and the steps dug in the hard snow beneath, and the creepers upon our feet gave good grip in it. Thus, slowly, step by step, we descended the ridge and in an hour and a half had reached the cleavage, the most critical place in the whole descent. With the least possible motion of the feet, setting them exactly in the shovelled steps, we crept like cats across this slope, thrusting the points of our axes into the holes that had been made in the ice-wall above, moving all together, the rope always taut, no one speaking a word. When once Karstens was anchored on the further ice he stood and gathered up the rope as first one and then another passed safely to him and anchored himself beside him, until at last we were all across. Then, stooping to pass the overhanging ice-cliff that here also disputed the pack upon one's back, we went down to the long, long stretch of jagged pinnacles and bergs, and our intricate staircase in the masonry of them. Shovelling was necessary all the way down, but the steps were there, needing only to be uncovered. Passing our ridge camp, passing the danger of the great gable, down the rocks by which we reached the ridge and down the slopes to the glacier floor we went, reaching our old camp at 9.30 P. M., six and a quarter hours from the Parker Pass, twelve hours from the eighteen-thousand-foot camp in the Grand Basin, our hearts full of thankfulness that the terrible ridge was behind us. Until we reached the glacier floor the weather had been clear; almost immediately thereafter the old familiar cloud smother began to pour down from above and we saw the heights no more.

The camp was in pretty bad shape. The snow that had fallen upon it had melted and frozen to ice, in the sun's rays and the night frosts, and weighed the tent down to the ground. But an hour's work made it habitable again, and we gleefully piled the stove with the last of our wood and used the last spoonfuls of a can of baking-powder to make a batch of biscuits, the first bread we had eaten in two weeks.

Next day we abandoned the camp, leaving all standing, and, putting our packs upon a Yukon sled, rejecting the ice-creepers, and resuming our rough-locked snow-shoes, we started down the glacier in soft, cloudy weather to our base camp. Again it had been wiser to have waited till night, that the snow bridges over the crevasses might be at their hardest; but we could not wait. Every mind was occupied with Johnny. We were two weeks overstayed of the time we had told him to expect our return, and we knew not what might have happened to the boy. The four of us on one rope, Karstens leading and Walter at the gee-pole, we went down the first sharp descents of the glaciers without much trouble, the new, soft snow making a good brake for the sled. But lower down the crevasses began to give us trouble. The snow bridges were melted at their edges, and sometimes the sled had to be lowered down to the portion that still held and hauled up at the other side. Sometimes a bridge gave way as its edge was cautiously ventured upon with the snow-shoes, and we had to go far over to the glacier wall to get round the crevasse. The willows with which we had staked the trail still stood, sometimes just their tips appearing above the new snow, and they were a good guide, though we often had to leave the old trail. At last the crevasses were all passed and we reached the lower portion of the glacier, which is free of them. Then the snow grew softer and softer, and our moccasined feet were soon wet through. Large patches of the black shale with which much of this glacier is covered were quite bare of snow, and the sled had to be hauled laboriously across them. Then we began to encounter pools of water, which at first we avoided, but they soon grew so numerous that we went right through them.

The going grew steadily wetter and rougher and more disagreeable. The lower stretch of a glacier is an unhandsome sight in summer: all sorts of rock débris and ugly black shale, with discolored melting ice and snow, intersected everywhere with streams of dirty water—this was what it had degenerated into as we reached the pass. The snow was entirely gone from the pass, so the sled was abandoned—left standing upright, with its gee-pole sticking in the air that if any one else ever chanced to want it it might readily be found. The snow-shoes were piled around it, and we resumed our packs and climbed up to the pass. The first thing that struck our eyes as we stood upon the rocks of the pass was a brilliant trailing purple moss flower of such gorgeous color that we all exclaimed at its beauty and wondered how it grew clinging to bare rock. It was the first bright color that we had seen for so long that it gave unqualified pleasure to us all and was a foretaste of the enhancing delights that awaited us as we descended to the bespangled valley. If a man would know to the utmost the charm of flowers, let him exile himself among the snows of a lofty mountain during fifty days of spring and come down into the first full flush of summer. We could scarcely pass a flower by, and presently had our hands full of blooms like schoolgirls on a picnic.

But although the first things that attracted our attention were the flowers, the next were the mosquitoes. They were waiting for us at the pass and they gave us their warmest welcome. The writer took sharp blame to himself that, organizing and equipping this expedition, he had made no provision against these intolerable pests. But we had so confidently expected to come out a month earlier, before the time of mosquitoes arrived, that although the matter was suggested and discussed it was put aside as unnecessary. Now there was the prospect of a fifty or sixty mile tramp across country, subject all the while to the assaults of venomous insects, which are a greater hindrance to summer travel in Alaska than any extremity of cold is to winter travel.

Not even the mosquitoes, however, took our minds from Johnny, and a load was lifted from every heart when we came near enough to our camp to see that some one was moving about it. A shout brought him running, and he never stopped until he had met us and had taken the pack from my shoulders and put it on his own. Our happiness was now unalloyed; the last anxiety was removed. The dogs gave us most jubilant welcome and were fat and well favored.

What a change had come over the place! All the snow was gone from the hills; the stream that gathered its three forks at this point roared over its rocks; the stunted willows were in full leaf; the

Johnny Fred who kept the base-camp and fed the dogs and would not touch the sugar.

thick, soft moss of every dark shade of green and yellow and red made a foil for innumerable brilliant flowers. The fat, gray conies chirped at us from the rocks; the ground-squirrels, greatly multiplied since the wholesale destruction of foxes, kept the dogs unavailingly chasing hither and thither whenever they were loose. We never grew tired of walking up and down and to and fro about the camp—it was a delight to tread upon the moss-covered earth after so long treading upon nothing but ice and snow; it was a delight to gaze out through naked eyes after all those weeks in which we had not dared even for a few moments to lay aside the yellow glasses in the open air; it was a delight to see joyful, eager animal life around us after our sojourn in regions dead. Supper was a delight. Johnny had killed four mountain-sheep and a caribou while we were gone, and not only had fed the dogs well, but from time to time had put aside choice portions expecting our return. But what was most grateful to us and most extraordinary in him, the boy had saved, untouched, the small ration of sugar and milk left for his consumption, knowing that ours was all destroyed; and we enjoyed coffee with these luxurious appurtenances as only they can who have been long deprived of them. There are not many boys of fifteen or sixteen of any race who would voluntarily have done the like.

The next day there was much to do. There were pack-saddles of canvas to make for the dogs' backs that they might help us carry our necessary stuff out; our own clothing and footwear to overhaul, bread to bake, guns to clean and oil against rust. Yet withal, we took it lazily, with five to divide these tasks, and napped and lay around and continually consumed biscuits and coffee which Johnny continually cooked. We all took at least a partial bath in the creek, cold as it was, the first bath in—well, in a long time. Mountain climbers belong legitimately to the great unwashed.

It was a day of perfect rest and contentment with hearts full of gratitude. Not a single mishap had occurred to mar the complete success of our undertaking—not an injury of any sort to any one, nor an illness. All five of us were in perfect health. Surely we had reason to be grateful; and surely we were happy in having Him to whom our gratitude might be poured out. What a bald, incomplete, and disconcerting thing it must be to have no one to thank for crowning mercies like these!

On Tuesday, the 10th June, we made our final abandonment, leaving the tent standing with stove and food and many articles that we did not need cached in it, and with four of the dogs carrying packs and led with chains, packs on our own backs and the ice-axes for staves in our hands, we turned our backs upon the mountain and went down the valley toward the Clearwater. The going was not too bad until we had crossed that stream and climbed the hills to the rolling country between it and the McKinley Fork of the Kantishna. Again and again we looked back for a parting glimpse of the mountain, but we never saw sign of it any more. The foot-hills were clear, the rugged wall of the glacier cut the sky, but the great mountain might have been a thousand miles off for any visible indication it gave. It is easy to understand how travellers across equatorial Africa have passed near the base of the snowy peaks of Ruwenzori without knowing they were even in the neighborhood of great mountains, and have come back and denied their existence.

The broken country between the streams was difficult. Underneath was a thick elastic moss in which the foot sank three or four inches at every step and that makes toilsome travelling. The mosquitoes were a constant annoyance. But the abundant bird life upon this open moorland, continually reminding one as it did of moorlands in the north of England or of Scotland, was full of interest. Ptarmigan, half changed from their snowy plumage to the brown of summer, and presenting a curious piebald appearance, were there in great numbers, cackling their guttural cry with its concluding notes closely resembling the "ko-ax, ko-ax" of the Frogs' Chorus in the comedy of Aristophanes; snipe whistled and curlews whirled all about us. Half-way across to the McKinley Fork it began to rain, thunder-peal succeeding thunder-peal, and each crash announcing a heavier downpour. Soon we were all wet through, and then the rain turned to hail that fell smartly until all the moss was white with it, and that gave place to torrents of rain again. Dog packs and men's packs were alike wet, and no one of us had a dry stitch on him when we reached the banks of the McKinley Fork and the old spacious hunting tent that stands there in which we were to spend the night. Rather hopelessly we hung our bedding to dry on ropes strung about some trees, and our wet clothing around the stove. By taking turns all the night in sitting up, to keep a fire going, we managed to get our clothes dried by morning, but the bedding was wet as ever. Fortunately, the night was a warm one.

The next morning there was the McKinley Fork

to cross the first thing, and it was a difficult and disagreeable task. This stream, which drains the Muldrow Glacier and therefore the whole north-east face of Denali, occupies a dreary, desolate bed of boulder and gravel and mud a mile or more wide; rather it does not occupy it, save perhaps after tremendous rain following great heat, but wanders amid it, with a dozen channels of varying depth but uniform blackness, the inky solution of the shale which the mountain discharges so abundantly tingeing not only its waters but the whole Kantishna, into which it flows one hundred miles away. Commonly in the early morning the waters are low, the night frosts checking the melting of the glacier ice; but this morning the drainage of yesterday's rain-storm had swollen them. Channel after channel was waded in safety until the main stream was reached, and that swept by, thigh-deep, with a rushing black current that had a very evil look. Karstens was scouting ahead, feeling for the shallower places, stemming the hurrying waters till they swept up to his waist. The dogs did not like the look of it and with their packs, still wet from yesterday, were hampered in swimming. Two that Tatum was leading suddenly turned back when half-way across, and the chains, entangling his legs, pulled him over face foremost into the deepest of the water. His pack impeded his efforts to rise, and the water swept all over him. Karstens hurried back to his rescue, and he was extricated from his predicament, half drowned and his clothes filled with mud and sand. There was no real danger of drowning, but it was a particularly noxious ducking in icy filth. The sun was warm, however, and after basking upon the rocks awhile he was able to proceed, still wet, though he had stripped and wrung out his clothes —for we had no dry change—and very gritty in underwear, but taking no harm whatever. I think Tatum regretted losing, in the mad rush of black water, the ice-axe he had carried to the top of the mountain more than he regretted his wetting.

On the further bank of the McKinley Fork we entered our first wood, a belt about three miles wide that lines the river. Our first forest trees gave us almost as much pleasure as our first flowers. Animal life abounded, all in the especially interesting condition of rearing half-grown young. Squirrels from their nests scolded at our intrusion most vehemently; an owl flew up with such a noisy snapping and chattering that our attention was drawn to the point from which she rose, and there, perched upon a couple of rotten stumps a few feet apart, were two half-fledged owlets, passive, immovable, which allowed themselves to be photographed and even handled without any indication of life except in their wondering eyes and the circumrotary heads that contained them. Moose signs and bear signs were everywhere; rabbits, now in their summer livery, flitted from bush to bush. That belt of wood was a zoological garden stocked with birds and mammals. And we rejoiced with them over their promising families and harmed none.

From the wood we rose again to the moorland—to the snipe and ptarmigan and curlews, some yet sitting upon belated eggs—to the heavy going of the moss and the yet heavier going of niggerhead. Our journey skirted a large lake picturesquely surrounded by hills, and we spoke of how pleasantly a summer lodge might be placed upon its shores were it not for the mosquitoes. The incessant leaping of fish, the occasional flight of fowl alone disturbed the perfect reflection of cliff and hill in its waters. At times we followed game trails along its margin; at times swampy ground made us seek the hillside.

Thus, slowly covering the miles that we had gone so quickly over upon the ice of the lake two months before, we reached Moose Creek and the miners' cabins at Eureka late at night and received warm welcome and most hospitable entertainment from Mr. Jack Hamilton. It was good to see men other than our own party again, good to sleep in a bed once more, good to regale ourselves with food long strange to our mouths. Here we had our first intimation of any happenings in the outside world for the past three months and sorrowed that Saint Sophia was still to remain a Mohammedan temple, and that the kindly King of Greece had been murdered. Here also Hamilton generously provided us with spare mosquito-netting for veils, and we found a package of canvas gloves I had ordered from Fairbanks long before, and so were protected from our chief enemies. From Moose Creek we went over the hills to Caribou Creek and again were most kindly welcomed and entertained by Mr. and Mrs. Quigley, and discussed our climb for a long while with McGonogill of the "pioneer" party. Then, mainly down the bed of Glacier Creek, now on lingering ice or snow-drift, with the water rushing underneath, now on the rocks, now through the brush, crossing and recrossing the creek, we reached the long line of desolate, decaying houses known as Glacier City, and found convenient refuge in one of the cabins therein, still maintained as an occasional abode. On the

"Muk," the author's pet malamute.

outskirts of the "city" next morning a moose and two calves sprang up from the brush, our approach over the moss not giving enough notice to awake her from sleep until we were almost upon her.

Instead of pursuing our way across the increasingly difficult and swampy country to the place where our boat and supplies lay cached, we turned aside at midday to the "fish camp" on the Bearpaw, and, after enjoying the best our host possessed from the stream and from his early garden, borrowed his boat, choosing twenty miles or so on the water to nine of niggerhead and marsh. But the river was very low and we had much trouble getting the boat over riffles and bars, so that it was late at night when we reached that other habitation of dragons known as Diamond City. While we submerged our cached poling boat to swell its sun-dried seams, Walter and Johnny returned the borrowed boat, and, since the stream had fallen yet more, were many hours in reaching the fish camp and in tramping back.

But the labor of the return journey was now done. A canvas stretched over willows made a shelter for the centre of the boat, and at noon on the second day men, dogs, and baggage were embarked, to float down the Bearpaw to the

Kantishna, to the Tanana, to the Yukon. The Bearpaw swarmed with animal life. Geese and ducks, with their little terrified broods, scooted ahead of us on the water, the mothers presently leaving their young in a nook of the bank and making a flying dĕtour to return to them. Sometimes a duck would simulate a broken wing to lure us away from the little ones. We had no meat and were hungry for the usual early summer diet of water-fowl, but not hungry enough to kill these birds. Beaver dropped noisily into the water from trees that exhibited their marvellous carpentry, some lying prostrate, some half chiselled through. It seemed, indeed, as though the beaver were preparing great irrigation works all through this country. Since the law went into effect prohibiting their capture until 1915 they have increased and multiplied all over interior Alaska. They are still caught by the natives, but since their skins cannot be sold the Indians are wearing beaver garments again to the great advantage of health in the severe winters. One wishes very heartily that the prohibition might be made perpetual, for only so will fur become the native wear again. It is good to see the children, particularly, in beaver coats and breeches instead of the wretched cotton that otherwise is almost their only garb. Would it be altogether beyond reason to hope that a measure which was enacted to prevent the extermination of an animal might be perpetuated on behalf of the survival of an interesting and deserving race of human beings now sorely threatened? Or is it solely the conservation of commercial resources that engages the attention of government? There are few measures that would redound more to the physical benefit of the Alaskan Indian than the perpetuating of the law against the sale of beaver skins. With the present high and continually appreciating price of skins, none of the common people of the land, white or native, can afford to wear furs. Such a prohibition as has been suggested would restore to Alaskans a small share in the resources of Alaska. Is there any country in the world where furs are actually needed more?

Not only beaver, but nearly all fur and game animals have greatly increased in the Kantishna country. In the year of the stampede, when thousands of men spent the winter here, there was wholesale destruction of game and trapping of fur. But the country, left to itself, is now re-stocked of game and fur, except of foxes, the high price of which has almost exterminated them here and is rapidly exterminating them throughout interior Alaska. They have been poisoned in the most reckless and unscrupulous way, and there seems no means of stopping it under the present law. We saw scarcely a fox track in the country, though a few years ago they were exceedingly plentiful all over the foot-hills of the great range. Mink, marten, and muskrat were seen from time to time swimming in the river; a couple of yearling moose started from the bank where they had been drinking as we noiselessly turned a bend; brilliant kingfishers flitted across the water. So down these rivers we drifted, sometimes in sunshine, sometimes in rain, until early in the morning of the 20th June, we reached Tanana, and our journey was concluded three months and four days after it was begun. When the telegraph office opened at 8 o'clock a message was sent, in accordance with promise, to a Seattle paper, and it illustrates the rapidity with which news is spread to-day that a ship in Bering Sea, approaching Nome, received the news from Seattle by wireless telegraph before 11 A. M. But a message from the Seattle paper received the same morning asking for "five hundred more words describing narrow escapes" was left unanswered, for, thank God, there were none to describe.

CHAPTER VII

THE HEIGHT OF DENALI, WITH A DISCUSSION OF THE READINGS ON THE SUMMIT AND DURING THE ASCENT

THE determination of the heights of mountains by triangulation is, of course, the method that in general commends itself to the topographer, though it may be questioned whether the very general use of aneroids for barometric determinations has not thrown this latter means of measuring altitudes into undeserved discredit when the mercurial barometer is used instead of its convenient but unreliable substitute.

The altitude given on the present maps for Denali is the mean of determinations made by triangulation by three different men: Muldrow on the Sushitna* side in 1898, Raeburn on the Kuskokwim side in 1902, and Porter, from the Yentna

* "Sushitna" represents unquestionably the native pronunciation and the "h" should be retained. The reason for its elision current in Alaska is too contemptible to be referred to further. Perhaps the same genius removed this "h" who removed the "'s" from the "Cook's Inlet" of the British admiralty. One is not surprised when

country in 1906. In addition, a determination was made by the Coast and Geodetic Survey in 1910, from points near Cook's Inlet. "The work of the Coast Survey," writes Mr. Alfred Brooks, "is more refined than the rough triangulation done by our men; at the same time they were much further away." "It is a curious coincidence," he adds, "that the determination made by the Coast Survey was the mean which we had assumed from our three determinations" (twenty thousand three hundred feet).

There are, however, two sources of error in the determination of the height of this mountain by triangulation—a general one and a particular one. The general one lies in the difficulty of ascertaining the proper correction to be applied for the refraction of the atmosphere, and the higher the mountain the greater the liability to this error; for not much is positively known about the angle of refraction of the upper regions of the air. The officers of the Trigonometrical Survey of India

a post-office at Cape Prince of Wales is named "Wales" because one is not surprised at any banalities of the postal department—in Alaska or elsewhere, but one expects better things from the cultured branches of the government service. It is interesting to speculate what will happen to Revillegigedo Island, which Vancouver named for the viceroy of Mexico who was kind to him, when the official curtailer of names finds time to attend to *it*. If there be a post-office thereon it is probably already named "Gig."

have published their opinion that the heights of the great peaks of the Himalayas will have to be revised on this account. The report of the Coast Survey's determination of the height of Denali claims a "co-efficient of refraction nearer the truth" than the figure used on a previous occasion; but a very slight difference in this factor will make a considerable difference in the result.

The particular source of error in the case of this mountain lies in the circumstance that its summit is flat, and there is no culminating point upon which the cross-hairs of the surveying instrument may intersect.

The barometric determination of heights is, of course, not without similar troubles of its own. The tables of altitudes corresponding to pressures do not agree, Airy's table giving relatively greater altitudes for very low pressures than the Smithsonian. All such tables as originally calculated are based upon the hypothesis of a temperature and humidity which decrease regularly with the altitude, and this is not always the case; nor is the "static equilibrium of the atmosphere" which Laplace assumed always maintained; that is to say an equal difference of pressure does not always correspond to an equal difference of altitude. There is, in point of fact, no absolute way to determine altitude save by running an actual line of levels; all other methods are approximations at best. But there had never been a barometric determination of the height of this mountain made, and it was resolved to attempt it on this expedition.

To this end careful arrangements were made and much labor and trouble undergone. The author carried his standard mercurial mountain barometer to Fort Gibbon on the Yukon in September, 1912, and compared it with the instrument belonging to the Signal Corps of the United States army at that post. A very close agreement was found in the two instruments; the reading of the one, by himself, and of the other, by the sergeant whose regular duty it was to read and record the instrument, being identical to two places of decimals at the same temperature.

Arrangements were made with Captain Michel of the Signal Corps at Fort Gibbon, when the expedition started to the mountain in March, 1913, to read the barometer at that post three times a day and record the reading with the reading of the attached thermometer. Acknowledgment is here made of Captain Michel's courtesy and kindness in this essential co-operation. The reading at Fort Gibbon which most nearly synchronizes with the reading on top of the mountain is the one taken at noon on the 7th June. The reading on top of the mountain was made at about 1.50 P. M., so that there was an hour and fifty minutes difference in time. The weather, however, was set fair, without a cloud in the sky, and had been for more than twelve hours before and remained so for thirty-six hours afterward. It would seem, therefore, that the difference in time is negligible. The reading at Fort Gibbon, a place of an altitude of three hundred and thirty-four feet above sea-level, at noon on the 7th June, was 29.590 inches with an attached thermometer reading 76.5° F. The reading on the summit of Denali, at 1.50 P. M. on the same day, was 13.617. The writer is greatly chagrined that he cannot give with the same confidence the reading of the attached thermometer on top of the mountain, but desires to set forth the circumstances and give the readings in his note-book records.

The note-book gives the air temperature on the summit as 7° F., taken by a standard alcohol minimum thermometer, and it remained constant during the hour and a half we were there. The sun was shining, but a bitter north wind was blowing. But the reading of the thermometer attached to the barometer is recorded as 20° F. I am unable to account for this discrepancy of 13°. The mercurial barometer was swung on its tripod inside the instrument tent we had carried to the summit, a rough zero was established, and it was left for twenty minutes or so to adjust itself to conditions before an exact reading was taken. It was my custom throughout the ascent to read and record the thermometer immediately after the barometer was read, but it is almost certain that on this momentous occasion it was not done. Possibly the thermometer was read immediately the instrument was taken out of its leather case and its wooden case and set up, while it yet retained some of the animal heat of the back that had borne it, and the reading was written in the prepared place. Then when the barometer was finally read, no temperature of the attached thermometer was noted. This is the only possible explanation that occurs, and it is very unsatisfactory. It was not until we were down at the base camp again that I looked at the figures, and discovered their difference, and I could not then recall in detail the precise operations on the summit. It is hard to understand, ordinarily, how any man could have recorded the two readings on the same page of the book without noticing their discrepancy, but perhaps the excitement and difficulty of the situation combined to produce what Sir Martin Conway calls "high altitude stupidity."

It is indeed impossible to convey to the reader who has never found himself circumstanced as we were an understanding of our perturbation of mind and body upon reaching the summit of the mountain: breathless with excitement—and with the altitude—hearts afire and feet nigh frozen. What should be done on top, what first, what next, had been carefully planned and even rehearsed, but we were none of us schooled in stoical self-repression to command our emotions completely. Here was the crown of nearly three months' toil—and of all those long years of desire and expectation. It was hard to gather one's wits and resolutely address them to prearranged tasks; hard to secure a sufficient detachment of mind for careful and accurate observations. The sudden outspreading of the great mass of Denali's Wife immediately below us and in front of us was of itself a surprise that was dramatic and disconcerting; a splendid vision from which it was difficult to withdraw the eyes. We knew, of course, the companion peak was there, but had forgotten all about her, having had no slightest glimpse of her on the whole ascent until at the one stroke she stood completely revealed. Not more dazzling to the eyes of the pasha in the picture was the form of the lovely woman when the slave throws off the draperies that veiled her from head to foot. Moreover, problems that had been discussed and disputed, questions about the conformation of the mountain and the possibilities of approach to it, were now soluble at a glance and clamored for solution. We held them back and fell at once to our scientific work, denying any gratification of sight until these tasks were performed, yet it is plain that I at least was not proof against the disturbing consciousness of the wonders that waited.

It was bitterly cold, yet my fingers, though numb, were usable when I reached the top; it was in exposing them to manipulate the hypsometrical instruments that they lost all feeling and came nigh freezing. And breathlessness was naturally at its worst; I remember that even the exertion of rising from the prone position it was necessary to assume to read the barometer brought on a fit of panting.

With these circumstances in mind we will resume the discussion of the readings taken on the summit and their bearing upon the altitude of the mountain. It seems right to disregard the temperature recorded for the attached thermometer, and to use the air temperature, of which there is no doubt, in correcting the barometric reading. So they stand:

Bar.	Temp.
13.617 inches	7° F.

The boiling-point thermometer stood at 174.9° F. when the steam was pouring out of the vent.

They stand therefore:

Gibbon (334 feet altitude)		*The Summit of Denali*	
Bar.	Ther.	Bar.	Ther.
29.590	76.5° F.	13.617	7° F.

Now, the tables accessible to the writer do not work out their calculations beyond eighteen thousand feet, and he confesses himself too long unused to mathematical labors of any kind for the task of extending them. He was, therefore, constrained to fall back upon the kindness of Mr. Alfred Brooks, the head of the Alaskan Division of the United States Geological Survey, and Mr. Brooks turned over the data to Mr. C. E. Giffin, topographic engineer of that service, to which gentleman thankful acknowledgment is made for the result that follows.

Ignoring a calculation based upon a temperature of 20° F. on the summit, and another based upon a temperature of 13.5° F. on the summit (the mean of the air temperature and that recorded for the attached thermometer) and confining attention to the calculation which takes the air temperature of 7° F. as the proper figure for the correction of the barometer, a result is reached which shows the summit of Denali as twenty-one thousand and eight feet above the sea. It should be added that Mr. Giffin obtained from the United States Weather Bureau the barometric and thermometric readings taken at Valdez on 7th June about the same length of time after our reading on the summit as the reading at Gibbon was before ours. From these readings Mr. Giffin makes the altitude of the mountain twenty thousand three hundred and seventy-four feet above Valdez, which is ten feet above the sea-level. From this result Mr. Giffin is disposed to question the accuracy of the reading at Gibbon, though the author has no reason to doubt it was properly and carefully made. Valdez is much farther from the summit than Fort Gibbon and is in a different climatic zone. The calculation from the Valdez base should, however, be taken into consideration in making this barometric determination, and the mean of the two results, twenty thousand six hundred and ninety-six feet, or, roundly, *twenty thousand seven hundred feet,* is offered as the contribution of this expedition toward determining the true altitude of the mountain.

The figures of Mr. Giffin's calculations touching the altitude of this mountain and also determining the altitudes of various salient points or stages of the ascent of the mountain are printed below:

DENALI (MOUNT McKINLEY)

USING AIR THERMOMETER READING +7° AND THE READING AT FORT GIBBON FOR SAME DATE

Mount McKinley, barometric reading...........................	13.617 in.	
Barometer reduced to standard temperature....................	+.027 "	Temp. 7°
	13.644 in.	
Fort Gibbon, barometric reading ..	29.590 in.	
Barometer reduced to standard temperature......................	−.128 "	Temp. 76.5°
	29.462 in.	
Mount McKinley, corrected barometer..........................	13.644 in.	21,324 ft.
Fort Gibbon, corrected barometer..	29.462 "	400 "
		20,924 ft.

Mean temperature, 41.7°—approximate difference in elevation......	20,924 ft.	−356 ft.
Latitude, 64°—approximate difference in elevation...............	20,568 "	+15 "
Mean temperature, 41.7°—approximate difference in elevation.....	20,568 "	+71 "
Elevation lowest, 400—approximate difference in elevation..........	20,568 "	+20 "
Elevation above Fort Gibbon...........		20,674 ft.
Elevation of Fort Gibbon..............		334 "
Elevation above sea.....................		21,008 ft.

Using the Thermometric Reading of 7° at Mount McKinley and the U. S. Weather Bureau Reading at Valdez for Same Date

Mount McKinley, barometric reading..........................	13.617 in.	
Barometer reduced to standard temperature......................	+.027 "	Temp. 7°
	13.644 in.	
Valdez, barometric reading........	29.76 in.	
Barometer reduced to standard temperature......................	.068 "	
	29.692 in.	Temp. 54°
Mount McKinley, corrected barometric reading.................	13.644 in.	21,324 ft.
Valdez, corrected barometric reading	29.692 "	190 "
		21,134 ft.
Mean temperature, 30.5°—approximate difference in elevation.....	21,134 ft.	−840 "
Latitude, 62°—approximate difference in elevation...............	20,295 "	+18 "

Mean temperature, 30.5°—approximate difference in elevation....	20,295 ft.	+42 ft.
Elevation lowest, 190—approximate difference in elevation..........	20,295 "	+20 "
Elevation above Valdez................		20,374 ft.
Elevation of Valdez..................		10 "
Elevation above sea....................		20,384 ft.

ALTITUDES OF CAMPING STATIONS

First Glacier Camp

Glacier Camp, barometric reading.	22.554 in.	Temp. 81°
Barometer reduced to standard temperature.....................	−.106 "	
	22.448 in.	
Fort Gibbon, barometric reading...	29.110 in.	Temp. 74°
Barometer reduced to standard temperature.....................	−.120 "	
	28.990 in.	
Glacier Camp, corrected barometer	22.448 in.	7,791 ft.
Fort Gibbon, corrected barometer..	28.990 "	840 "
		6,951 ft.
Mean temperature, 77.5°—approximate difference in elevation.....	6,951 ft.	+393 "
Latitude, 64°—approximate difference in elevation...............	7,343 "	+5 "
Mean temperature, 77.5°—approximate difference in elevation.....	7,343 "	+74 "
Elevation lowest, 840—approximate difference in elevation..........	7,343 "	+3 "
Elevation above Fort Gibbon...........		7,426 ft.
Elevation of Fort Gibbon..............		334 "
Elevation above sea....................		7,760 ft.

Head of Muldrow Glacier

Muldrow Glacier, barometric reading	19.640 in. Temp. 36°	
Barometer reduced to standard temperature	−.013 "	
	19.627 in.	
Fort Gibbon, barometric reading	30.065 in. Temp. 71°	
Barometer reduced to standard temperature	−.115 "	
	29.950 in.	
Muldrow Glacier, corrected barometer	19.627 in.	11,441 ft.
Fort Gibbon, corrected barometer	29.950 "	(−)45 "
		11,486 ft.
Temperature, 53.5°—approximate difference in elevation	11,486 ft.	+79 "
Latitude, 65°—approximate difference in elevation	11,565 "	+8 "
Mean temperature, 53.5°—approximate difference in elevation	11,565 "	+63 "
Elevation lowest, 45—approximate difference in elevation	11,565 "	+6 "
Elevation above Fort Gibbon		11,642 ft.
Elevation of Fort Gibbon		334 "
Elevation above sea		11,976 ft.

Parker Pass

Parker Pass, barometric reading	17.330 in. Temp. 43°	
Barometer reduced to standard temperature	−.023 "	
	17.307 in.	

Fort Gibbon and Valdez as Bases

Fort Gibbon, barometric reading . .	30.050 in.	Temp. 69.5°
Barometer reduced to standard temperature	−.111 "	
	29.939 in.	
Parker Pass, corrected barometer. . .	17.307 in.	14,861 ft.
Fort Gibbon, corrected barometer . .	29.939 "	(−)35 "
		14,896 ft.
Mean temperature, 56.25°—approximate difference in elevation	14,896 ft.	+185 "
Latitude, 64°—approximate difference in elevation	15,091 "	+11 "
At temperature of 56.25°—approximate difference in elevation	15,091 "	+92 "
Elevation lowest, −35°—approximate difference in elevation	15,091 "	+11 "
Elevation above Fort Gibbon		15,195 ft.
Elevation of Fort Gibbon		334 "
Elevation above sea		15,529 ft.

Last Camp

Last Camp, barometric reading. . . .	15.220 in.	Temp. 40°
Barometer reduced to standard temperature	−.016 "	
	15.204 in.	
Fort Gibbon, barometric reading. . .	29.660 in.	
Barometer reduced to standard temperature	−.120 "	Temp. 73.5°
	29.540 in.	
Last Camp, corrected barometer. . .	15.204 in.	18,382 ft.
Fort Gibbon, corrected barometer. .	29.540 "	329 "
		18,053 ft.

Mean temperature, 56.75°—approximate difference in elevation.....	18,053 ft.	+248 ft.
Latitude, 64°—approximate difference in elevation...............	18,301 "	+17 "
Mean temperature, 56.75°—approximate difference in elevation.....	18,301 "	+112 "
Elevation lowest, 329—approximate difference in elevation..........	18,301 "	+16 "
Elevation above Fort Gibbon...........		18,446 ft.
Elevation of Fort Gibbon..............		334 "
Elevation above sea......................		18,780 ft.

CHAPTER VIII

EXPLORATIONS OF THE DENALI REGION AND PREVIOUS ATTEMPTS AT ITS ASCENT

THE first mention in literature of the greatest mountain group in North America is in the narrative of that most notable navigator, George Vancouver. While surveying the Knik Arm of Cook's Inlet, in 1794, he speaks of his view of a connected mountain range "bounded by distant stupendous snow mountains covered with snow and apparently detached from each other." Vancouver's name has grown steadily greater during the last fifty years as modern surveys have shown the wonderful detailed accuracy of his work, and the seamen of the Alaskan coast speak of him as the prince of all navigators.

Not until 1878 is there another direct mention of these mountains, although the Russian name for Denali, "Bulshaia Gora," proves that it had long been observed and known.

In that year two of the early Alaskan traders,

Alfred Mayo and Arthur Harper, made an adventurous journey some three hundred miles up the Tanana River, the first ascent of that river by white men, and upon their return reported finding gold in the bars and mentioned an enormous ice mountain visible in the south, which they said was one of the most remarkable things they had seen on their trip.

In 1889 Frank Densmore, a prospector, with several companions, crossed from the Tanana to the Kuskokwim by way of the Coschaket and Lake Minchúmina, and had the magnificent view of the Denali group which Lake Minchúmina affords, which the present writer was privileged to have in 1911. Densmore's description was so enthusiastic that the mountain was known for years among the Yukon prospectors as "Densmore's mountain."

Though unquestionably many men traversed the region after the discovery of gold in Cook's Inlet in 1894, no other public recorded mention of the great mountain was made until W. A. Dickey, a Princeton graduate, journeyed extensively in the Sushitna and Chulitna valleys in 1896 and reached the foot of the glacier which drains one of the flanks of Denali, called later by Doctor Cook the Ruth Glacier. Dickey described the mountain in a letter to the New York *Sun* in January, 1907, and guessed its height with remarkable accuracy at twenty thousand feet. Probably unaware that the mountain had any native name, Dickey gave it the name of the Republican candidate for President of the United States at that time—McKinley. Says Mr. Dickey: "We named our great peak Mount McKinley, after William McKinley, of Ohio, the news of whose nomination for the presidency was the first we received on our way out of that wonderful wilderness."

In 1898 George Eldridge and Robert Muldrow, of the United States Geological Survey, traversed the region, and Muldrow estimated the height of the mountain by triangulation at twenty thousand three hundred feet.

In 1899 Lieutenant Herron crossed the range from Cook's Inlet and reached the Kuskokwim. It was he who named the lesser mountain of the Denali group, always known by the natives as Denali's Wife, "Mount Foraker," after the senator from Ohio.

In 1902 Alfred Brooks and D. L. Raeburn made a remarkable reconnoissance survey from the Pacific Ocean, passing through the range and along the whole western and northwestern faces of the group. They were the first white men to set foot upon the slopes of Denali. Shortly afterward, in response to the interest this journey aroused among Alpine clubs, Mr. Brooks published a pamphlet setting forth what he considered the most feasible plan for attempting the ascent of the mountain.

The next year saw two actual attempts at ascent. After holding the first term of court at Fairbanks, the new town on the Tanana River that had sprung suddenly into importance as the metropolis of Alaska upon the discovery of the Tanana gold-fields, Judge Wickersham (now delegate to Congress) set out with four men and two mules in May, 1903, and by steamboat ascended to the head of navigation of the Kantishna. Heading straight across an unknown country for the base of the mountain, Judge Wickersham's party unfortunately attacked the mountain by the Peters Glacier and demonstrated the impossibility of that approach, being stopped by the enormous ice-incrusted cliffs of the North Peak. Judge Wickersham used to say that only by a balloon or a flying-machine could the summit be reached; and, indeed, by no other means can the summit ever be reached from the north face. After a week spent in climbing, provisions began to run short and the party returned, descending the rushing, turbid waters of that quite unnavigable and very dangerous stream, the McKinley Fork of the Kantishna, on a raft, with little of anything left to eat, and that little damaged by water. Judge Wickersham was always keen for another attempt and often discussed the matter with the writer, but his judicial and political activities thenceforward occupied his time and attention to the exclusion of such enterprises. His attempt was the first ever made to climb the mountain.

Doctor Cook's Attempts

About the time that Judge Wickersham was leaving the north face of the mountain an expedition under Doctor Frederick A. Cook set out from Tyonek, on Cook's Inlet, on the other side of the range. Doctor Cook was accompanied by Robert Dunn, Ralph Shainwald (the "Hiram" of Dunn's narrative), and Fred Printz, who had been chief packer for Brooks and Raeburn, and fourteen pack-horses bore their supplies. The route followed was that of Brooks and Raeburn, and they had the advantage of topographical maps and forty miles of trail cut in the timber and a guide familiar with the country. Going up the Beluga and down the Skwentna Rivers, they crossed the range by the Simpson Pass to the south fork of the Kuskokwim, and then skirted the base of the mountains until a southwesterly ridge was reached which it is not very easy to locate, but which, as Doctor Brooks judges, must have been near the headwaters of the Tatlathna, a tributary of the Kuskokwim. Here an attempt was made to ascend the mountain, but at eight thousand feet a chasm cut them off from further advance.

Pursuing their northeast course, they reached the Peters Glacier (which Doctor Cook calls the Hanna Glacier) and stumbled across one of Judge Wickersham's camps of a couple of months before. Here another attempt to ascend was made, only to find progress stopped by the same stupendous cliffs that had turned back the Wickersham party. "Over the glacier which comes from the gap between the eastern and western peaks" (the North and South Peaks as we speak of them), says Doctor Cook, "there was a promising route." That is, indeed, part of the only route, but it can be reached only by the Muldrow Glacier. "The walls of the main mountain rise out of the Hanna (Peters) Glacier," Cook adds. The "main mountain" has many walls; the walls by which the summit alone may be reached rise out of the Muldrow Glacier, a circumstance that was not to be discovered for some years yet.

The lateness of the season now compelled immediate return. Passing still along the face of the range in the same direction, the party crossed the terminal moraine of the Muldrow Glacier without recognizing that it affords the only highway to the heart of the great mountain and recrossed the range by an ice-covered pass to the waters of the Chulitna River, down which they rafted after abandoning their horses. Doctor Cook calls this pass "Harper Pass," and the name should stand, for Cook was probably the first man ever to use it.

The chief result of this expedition, besides the exploration of about one hundred miles of unknown country, was the publication by Robert Dunn of an extraordinary narrative in several consecutive numbers of *Outing*, afterward republished in book form, with some modifications, as "The Shameless Diary of an Explorer," a vivid but unpleasant production, for which every squabble and jealousy of the party furnishes literary material. The book has a curious, undeniable power, despite its brutal frankness and its striving after "the poor renown of being smart," and it may live. One is thankful, however, that it is unique in the literature of travel.

Three years later Doctor Cook organized an expedition for a second attempt upon the mountain. In May, 1906, accompanied by Professor Herschel Parker, Mr. Belmore Browne, a topographer named Porter, who made some valuable maps, and packers, the party landed at the head of Cook's Inlet and penetrated by motor-boat and by pack-train into the Sushitna country, south of the range. Failing to cross the range at the head of the Yentna, they spent some time in explorations along the Kahilitna River, and, finding no avenue of approach to the heights of the mountain, the party returned to Cook's Inlet and broke up.

With only one companion, a packer named Edward Barrille, Cook returned in the launch up the Chulitna River to the Tokositna late in August. "We had already changed our mind as to the impossibility of climbing the mountain," he writes. Ascending a glacier which the Tokositna River drains, named by Cook the Ruth Glacier, they reached the amphitheatre at the glacier head. From this point, "up and up to the heaven-scraped granite of the top," Doctor Cook grows grandiloquent and vague, for at this point his true narrative ends.

The claims that Doctor Cook made upon his

Approaching the range.

return are well known, but it is quite impossible to follow his course from the description given in his book, "To the Top of the Continent." This much may be said: from the summit of the mountain, on a clear day, it seemed evident that no ascent was possible from the south side of the range at all. That was the judgment of all four members of our party. Doctor Cook talks about "the heaven-scraped granite of the top" and "the dazzling whiteness of the frosted granite blocks," and prints a photograph of the top showing granite slabs. There is no rock of any kind on the South (the higher) Peak above nineteen thousand feet. The last one thousand five hundred feet of the mountain is all permanent snow and ice; nor is the conformation of the summit in the least like the photograph printed as the "top of Mt. McKinley." In his account of the view from the summit he speaks of "the ice-blink caused by the extensive glacial sheets north of the Saint Elias group," which would surely be out of the range of any possible vision, but does not mention at all the master sight that bursts upon the eye when the summit is actually gained—the great mass of "Denali's Wife," or Mount Foraker, filling all the middle distance. We were all agreed that no one who had ever stood on the top of

Denali in clear weather could fail to mention the sudden splendid sight of this great mountain.

But it is not worth while to pursue the subject further. The present writer feels confident that any man who climbs to the top of Denali, and then reads Doctor Cook's account of his ascent, will not need Edward Barrille's affidavit to convince him that Cook's narrative is untrue. Indignation is, however, swallowed up in pity when one thinks upon the really excellent pioneering and exploring work done by this man, and realizes that the immediate success of the imposition about the ascent of Denali doubtless led to the more audacious imposition about the discovery of the North Pole—and that to his discredit and downfall.

The Pioneer Ascent

Although Cook's claim to have reached the summit of Denali met with general acceptance outside, or at least was not openly scouted, it was otherwise in Alaska. The men, in particular, who lived and worked in the placer-mining regions about the base of the mountain, and were, perhaps, more familiar with the orography of the range than any surveyor or professed topographer, were openly incredulous. Upon the appearance of Doctor Cook's book, "To the Top of the Continent," in 1908, the writer well remembers the eagerness with which his copy (the only one in Fairbanks) was perused by man after man from the Kantishna diggings, and the acute way in which they detected the place where vague "fine writing" began to be substituted for definite description.

Some of these men, convinced that the ascent had never been made, conceived the purpose of proving it in the only way in which it could be proved—by making the ascent themselves. They were confident that an enterprise which had now baffled several parties of "scientists," equipped with all sorts of special apparatus, could be accomplished by Alaskan "sourdoughs" with no special equipment at all. There seems also to have entered into the undertaking a naïve notion that in some way or other large money reward would follow a successful ascent.

The enterprise took form under Thomas Lloyd, who managed to secure the financial backing of McPhee and Petersen, saloon-keepers of Fairbanks, and Griffin, a wholesale liquor dealer of Chena. These three men are said to have put up five hundred dollars apiece, and the sum thus raised sufficed for the needs of the party. In February, 1910, therefore, Thomas Lloyd, Charles McGonogill, William Taylor, Peter Anderson, and Bob Horne, all experienced prospectors and miners, and E. C. Davidson, a surveyor, now the surveyor-general of Alaska, set out from Fairbanks, and by 1st March had established a base camp at the mouth of Cache Creek, within the foot-hills of the range.

Here Davidson and Horne left the party after a disagreement with Lloyd. The loss of Davidson was a fatal blow to anything beyond a "sporting" ascent, for he was the only man in the party with any scientific bent, or who knew so much as the manipulation of a photographic camera.

The Lloyd expedition was the first to discover the only approach by which the mountain may be climbed. Mr. Alfred Brooks, Mr. Robert Muldrow, and Doctor Cook had passed the snout of the Muldrow Glacier without realizing that it turned and twisted and led up until it gave access to the ridge by which alone the upper glacier or Grand Basin can be reached and the summits gained. From observations while hunting mountain-sheep upon the foot-hills for years past, Lloyd had already satisfied himself of this prime fact; had found the key to the complicated orography of the great mass. Lloyd had previously crossed the range with horses in this neighborhood by an easy pass that led "from willows to willows" in eighteen miles. Pete Anderson had come into the Kantishna country this way and had crossed and recrossed the range by this pass no less than eleven times.

McGonogill, following quartz leads upon the high mountains of Moose Creek, had traced from his aerie the course of the Muldrow Glacier, and had satisfied himself that within the walls of that glacier the route would be found. And, indeed, when he had us up there and pointed out the long stretch of the parallel walls it was plain to us also that they held the road to the heights. From the point where he had perched his tiny hut, a stone's throw from his tunnel, how splendidly the mountain rose and the range stretched out!

These men thus started with the great advantage of a knowledge of the mountain, and their plan for climbing it was the first that contained the possibility of success.

From the base camp Anderson and McGonogill scouted among the foot-hills of the range for some time before they discovered the pass that gives easy access to the Muldrow Glacier. On 25th March the party had traversed the glacier and reached its head with dogs and supplies. A camp was made on the ridge, while further prospecting was carried on toward the upper glacier. This was the farthest point that Lloyd reached. On 10th April, Taylor, Anderson, and McGonogill set out about two in the morning with great climbing-irons strapped to their moccasins and hooked pike-poles in their hands. Disdaining the rope and cutting no steps, it was "every man for himself," with reliance solely upon the *crampons*. They went up the ridge to the Grand Basin, crossed the ice to the North Peak, and proceeded to climb it, carrying the fourteen-foot flagstaff with them. Within perhaps five hundred feet of the summit, McGonogill, outstripped by Taylor and Anderson, and fearful of the return over the slippery ice-incrusted rocks if he went farther, turned back, but Taylor and Anderson reached the top (about twenty thousand feet above the sea) and firmly planted the flagstaff, which is there yet.

This is the true narrative of a most extraordinary feat, unique—the writer has no hesitation in claiming—in all the annals of mountaineering. He has been at the pains of talking with every member of the actual climbing party with a view to sifting the matter thoroughly.

For, largely by the fault of these men themselves, through a mistaken though not unchivalrous sense of loyalty to the organizer of the expedition, much incredulity was aroused in Alaska touching their exploit. It was most unfortunate that any mystery was made about the details, most unfortunate that in the newspaper accounts false claims were set up. Surely the merest common sense should have dictated that in the account of an ascent undertaken with the prime purpose of proving that Doctor Cook had *not* made the ascent, and had falsified his narrative, everything should be frank and aboveboard; but it was not so.

A narrative, gathered from Lloyd himself and agreed to by the others, was reduced to writing by Mr. W. E. Thompson, an able journalist of Fairbanks, and was sold to a newspaper syndicate. The account the writer has examined was "featured" in the New York Sunday *Times* of the 5th June, 1910.

In that account Lloyd is made to claim unequivocally that he himself reached both summits of the mountain. "There were two summits and we climbed them both"; and again, "When I reached the coast summit" are reported in quotation marks as from his lips. As a matter of fact, Lloyd himself reached neither summit, nor was much above the glacier floor; and the south or coast summit, the higher of the two, was not attempted by the party at all. There is no question that the party *could* have climbed the South Peak, though by reason of its greater distance it is safe to say that it could not have been reached, as the North Peak was, in one march from the ridge camp. It must have involved a camp in the Grand Basin with all the delay and the labor of relaying the stuff up there. But the men who accomplished the astonishing feat of climbing the North Peak, in one almost superhuman march from the saddle of the Northeast Ridge, could most certainly have climbed the South Peak too.

They did not attempt it for two reasons, first, because they wanted to plant their fourteen-foot flagstaff where it could be seen through a telescope from Fairbanks, one hundred and fifty miles away, as they fondly supposed, and, second, because not until they had reached the summit of the North Peak did they realize that the South Peak is higher. They told the writer that upon their return to the floor of the *upper* glacier they were greatly disappointed to find that their flagstaff was not visible to them. It is, indeed, only just visible with the naked eye from certain points on the upper glacier and quite invisible at any lower or more distant point. Walter Harper has particularly keen sight, and he was well up in the Grand Basin, at nearly seventeen thousand feet altitude, sitting and scanning the sky-line of the North Peak, seeking for the pole, when he caught sight of it and pointed it out. The writer was never sure that he saw it with the naked eye, though Karstens and Tatum did so as soon as Walter pointed it out, but through the field-glasses it was plain and prominent and unmistakable.

When we came down to the Kantishna diggings and announced to the men who planted it that we had seen the flagstaff, there was a feeling expressed that the climbing party of the previous summer must have seen it also and had suppressed mention of it; but there is no ground whatever for such a damaging assumption. It would never be seen with the naked eye save by those who were intently searching for it. Professor Parker and Mr. Belmore Browne entertained the pretty general incredulity about the "Pioneer" ascent, perhaps too readily, certainly too confidently; but the men themselves must bear the chief blame for that. The writer and his party, knowing these men much better, had never doubt that *some* of them had accomplished what was claimed, and these details have been gone into for no other reason than that honor may at last be given where honor is due.

To Lloyd belongs the honor of conceiving and organizing the attempt but not of accomplishing it. To him probably also belongs the original discovery of the route that made the ascent possible. To McGonogill belongs the credit of discovering the pass, probably the only pass, by which the glacier may be reached without following it from its snout up, a long and difficult journey; and to him also the credit of climbing some nineteen thousand five hundred feet, or to within five hundred feet of the North Peak. But to Pete Anderson and Billy Taylor, two of the strongest men, physically, in all the North, and to none other, belongs the honor of the first ascent of the North Peak and the planting of what must assuredly be the highest flagstaff in the world. The North Peak has never since been climbed or attempted.

. . . .

In the summer of the same year, 1910, Professor Parker and Mr. Belmore Browne, members of the second Cook party, convinced by this time that Cook's claim was wholly unfounded, attempted the mountain again, and another party, organized by Mr. C. E. Rust, of Portland, Oregon, also endeavored the ascent. But both these expeditions confined themselves to the hopeless southern side of the range, from which, in all probability, the mountain never can be climbed.

The Parker–Browne Expedition

To a man living in the interior of Alaska, aware of the outfitting and transportation facilities which the large commerce of Fairbanks affords, aware of the navigable waterways that penetrate close to the foot-hills of the Alaskan range, aware also of the amenities of the interior slope with its dry, mild climate, its abundance of game and rich pasturage compared with the trackless, lifeless snows of the coast slopes, there seems a strange fatuity in the persistent efforts to approach the mountain from the southern side of the range.

It is morally certain that if the only expedition that remains to be dealt with—that organized by Professor Parker and Mr. Belmore Browne in 1912, which came within an ace of success—had approached the mountain from the interior instead of from the coast, it would have forestalled us and accomplished the first complete ascent.

The difficulties of the coast approach have been described graphically enough by Robert Dunn in the summer and by Belmore Browne himself in the winter. There are no trails; the snow lies deep and loose and falls continually, or else the whole country is bog and swamp. There is no game.

The Parker-Browne expedition left Seward, on Resurrection Bay, late in January, 1912, and after nearly three months' travel, relaying their stuff forward, they crossed the range under extreme difficulties, being seventeen days above any vegetation, and reached the northern face of the mountain on 25th March. The expedition either missed the pass near the foot of the Muldrow Glacier, well known to the Kantishna miners, by which it is possible to cross from willows to willows in eighteen miles, or else avoided it in the vain hope of finding another. They then went to the Kantishna diggings and procured supplies and topographical information from the miners, and were thus able to follow the course of the Lloyd party of 1910, reaching the Muldrow Glacier by the gap in the glacier wall discovered by McGonogill and named McPhee Pass by him.

Mr. Belmore Browne has written a lucid and stirring account of the ascent which his party made. We were fortunate enough to secure a copy of the magazine in which it appeared just before leaving Fairbanks, and he had been good enough to write a letter in response to our inquiries and to enclose a sketch map. Our course was almost precisely the same as that of the Parker-Browne party up to seventeen thousand feet, and the course of that party was precisely the same as that of the Lloyd party up to fifteen thousand feet. There is only one way up the mountain, and Lloyd and his companions discovered it. The earthquake had enormously increased the labor of the ascent; it had not altered the route.

A reconnoissance of the Muldrow Glacier to its head and a long spell of bad weather delayed the party so much that it was the 4th June before the actual ascent was begun—a very late date indeed; more than a month later than our date and nearly three months later than the "Pioneer" date. It is rarely that the mountain is clear after the 1st June; almost all the summer through its summit is wrapped in cloud. From the junction of the Tanana and Yukon Rivers it is often visible for weeks at a time during the winter, but is rarely seen at all after the ice goes out. A close watch kept by friends at Tanana (the town at the confluence of the rivers) discovered the summit on the day we reached it and the following day (the 7th and 8th June) but not for three weeks before and not at all afterward; from which it does not follow, however, that the summit was not visible momentarily, or at certain hours of the day, but only that it was not visible for long enough to be observed. The rapidity with which that summit shrouds and clears itself is sometimes marvellous.

As is well known, the Parker-Browne party pushed up the Northeast Ridge and the upper glacier and made a first attack upon the summit itself, from a camp at seventeen thousand feet, on the 29th June. When within three or four hundred feet of the top they were overwhelmed and driven down, half frozen, by a blizzard that suddenly arose. On the 1st July another attempt was made, but the clouds ascended and completely enveloped the party in a cold, wind-driven mist so that retreat to camp was again imperative. Only those who have experienced bad weather at great heights can understand how impossible it is to proceed in the face of it. The strongest, the hardiest, the most resolute must yield. The party could linger no longer; food supplies were exhausted. They broke camp and went down the mountain.

The falling short of complete success of this very gallant mountaineering attempt seems to have been due, first to the mistake of approaching the mountain by the most difficult route, so that it was more than five months after starting that the actual climbing began; or, if the survey made justified, and indeed decided, the route, then the summit was sacrificed to the survey. But the immediate cause of the failure was the mistake of relying upon canned pemmican for the main food supply. This provision, hauled with infinite labor from the coast, and carried on the backs of the party to the high levels of the mountain, proved uneatable and useless at the very time when it was depended upon for subsistence. There is no finer big-game country in the world than that around the interior slopes of the Alaskan range; there is no finer meat in the world than caribou and mountain-sheep. It is carrying coals to Newcastle to bring canned meat into this country—nature's own larder stocked with her choicest supplies. But if, attempting the mountain when they did, the Parker-Browne party had remained two or three days longer in the Grand Basin, which they would assuredly have done had their food been eatable, their bodies would be lying up there yet or would be crushed beneath the débris of the earthquake on the ridge.

CHAPTER IX

THE NAMES PLACED UPON THE MOUNTAIN BY THE AUTHOR

THERE was no intent of putting names at all upon any portions of this mountain when the expedition was undertaken, save that the author had it in his mind to honor the memory of a very noble and very notable gentlewoman who gave ten years of her life to the Alaskan natives, set on foot one of the most successful educational agencies in the interior, and died suddenly and heroically at her post of duty a few years since, leaving a broad and indelible mark upon the character of a generation of Indians. Miss Farthing lies buried high up on the bluffs opposite the school at Nenana, in a spot she was wont to visit for the fine view of Denali it commands, and her brother, the present bishop of Montreal, and some of her colleagues of the Alaskan mission, have set a concrete cross there. When we entered the Alaskan range by Cache Creek there rose directly before us a striking pyramidal peak, some twelve or thirteen thousand feet high. Not knowing that any name had been bestowed upon it, the author discharged himself of the duty that he conceived lay upon him of associating Miss Farthing's name permanently with the mountain range she loved and the country in which she labored. But he has since learned that Professor Parker placed upon this mountain, a year before, the name of Alfred Brooks, of the Alaskan Geological Survey. Apart from the priority of naming, to which, of course, he would immediately yield, the author knows of no one whose name should so fitly be placed upon a peak of the Alaskan range, and he would himself resist any effort to change it.

Having gratified this desire, as he supposed, there had meantime arisen another desire,—upon reading the narrative of the Parker-Browne expedition of the previous year, a copy of which we were fortunate enough to procure just as we were starting for the mountain. It was the feeling of our whole company that the names of Professor Parker and Mr. Belmore Browne should be associated with the mountain they so very nearly ascended.

When the eyes are cast aloft from the head of the Muldrow Glacier the most conspicuous feature of the view is a rudely conical tower of granite, standing sentinel over the entrance to the Grand Basin, and at the base of that tower is the pass into the upper glacier which is, indeed, the key of the whole ascent of the mountain. (See illustration opposite p. 40.)

We found no better place to set these names; we called the tower the Browne Tower and the pass the Parker Pass. The "pass" may not, it is true, conform to any strict Alpine definition of that term, but it gives the only access to the glacier floor. From the ridge below to the glacier above this place gives passage; and any place that gives passage may broadly be termed a pass.

It was when this pass had been reached, after three weeks' toil, that the author was moved to the bestowal of another name by his admiration for the skill and pluck and perseverance of his chief colleague in the ascent. Those who think that a long apprenticeship must be served under skilled instructors before command of the technique of snow mountaineering can be obtained would have been astonished at Karstens's work on the Northeast Ridge. But it must be kept in mind that, while he had no previous experience on the heights, he had many years of experience with ice and snow—which is true of all of us except Tatum, and *he* had two winters' experience. In the course of winter travel in the interior of Alaska most of the problems of snow mountaineering present themselves at one time or another.

The designation "Northeast," which the Parker-Browne party put upon the ridge that affords passage from the lower glacier to the upper, is open to question. Mr. Charles Sheldon, who spent a year around the base of the mountain studying the fauna of the region, refers to the *outer* wall of the Muldrow Glacier as the Northeast Ridge, that is, the wall that rises to the North Peak. Perhaps "East Ridge of the South Peak" would be the most exact description. But it is here proposed to substitute Harry Karstens's name for points-of-the-compass designations, and call the ridge, part of which the earthquake shattered, the dividing ridge between the two arms of the Muldrow Glacier, soaring tremendously and impressively with ice-incrusted cliffs in its lower course, the Karstens Ridge. Regarded in its whole extent, it is one of the capital features of the mountain. It is seen to the left in the picture opposite page 26, where Karstens stands alone. At this point of its course it soars to its greatest elevation, five or six thousand feet above the glacier floor; it is seen again in the middle distance of the picture opposite page 164.

Not until this book was in preparation and the author was digging into the literature of the mountain did he discover the interesting connection of Arthur Harper, father of Walter Harper, narrated in another place, with Denali, and not until that discovery did he think of suggesting the name Harper for any feature of the mountain, despite the distinction that fell to the young man of setting the first foot upon the summit. Then the upper glacier appeared to be the most appropriate place for the name, and, after reflection, it is deemed not improper to ask that this glacier be so known.

It has thus fallen out that each of the author's colleagues is distinguished by some name upon the mountain except Robert Tatum. But to Tatum belongs the honor of having raised the stars and stripes for the first time upon the highest point in all the territory governed by the United States; and he is well content with that distinction. Keen as the keenest amongst us to reach the top, Tatum had none the less been entirely willing to give it up and go down to the base camp and let Johnny take his place (when he was unwell at the head of the glacier owing to long confinement in the tent during bad weather), if in the judgment of the writer that had been the wisest course for the whole party. Fortunately the indisposition passed, and the matter is referred to only as indicating the spirit of the man. I suppose there is no money that could buy from him the little silk flag he treasures.

It was also while this book was preparing that the author found that he had unwittingly renamed Mount Brooks, and the prompt withdrawal of his suggested name for that peak left the one original desire of naming a feature of the mountain or the range ungratified, and his obligation toward a revered memory unfulfilled.

Where else might that name be placed? For a long time no place suggested itself; then it was called to mind that the two horns at the extremities of the horseshoe ridge of the South Peak were unnamed. Here were twin peaks, small, yet lofty and conspicuous—part of the main summit of the mountain. The naming of one almost carried with it the naming of the other; and as soon as the name Farthing alighted, so to speak, from his mind upon the one, the name Carter settled itself upon the other. In the long roll of women who have labored devotedly for many years amongst the natives of the interior of Alaska, there are no brighter names than those of Miss Annie Farthing and Miss Clara Carter, the one forever associated with Nenana, the other with the Allakaket. To those who are familiar with what has been done and what is doing for the Indians of the interior, to the white men far and wide who have owed recovery of health and relief and refreshment to the ministrations of these capable women, this naming will need no labored justification; and if self-sacrifice and love, and tireless, patient labor for the good of others be indeed the greatest things in the world, then the mountain top bearing aloft these names does not so much do honor as is itself dignified and ennobled. These horns of the South Peak are shown in the picture opposite page 96; they are of almost equal height; the near one the author would name the Farthing Horn, the far one the Carter Horn.

And now the author finds that he has done what, in the past, he has faulted others for doing —he has plastered a mountain with names. The prerogative of name-giving is a dangerous one, without definite laws or limitations. Nothing but common consent and usage ultimately establish names, but he to whom falls the first exploration of a country, or the first ascent of a peak, is usually accorded privilege of nomenclature. Yet it is a privilege that is often abused and should be exercised with reserve. Whether or not it has been overdone in the present case, others must say. This, however, the author will say, and would say as emphatically as is in his power: that he sets no store whatever by the names he has ventured to confer comparable with that which he sets by the restoration of the ancient native names of the whole great mountain and its companion peak.

It may be that the Alaskan Indians are doomed; it may be that the liquor and disease which to-day are working havoc amongst them will destroy them off the face of the earth; it is common to meet white men who assume it with complacency. Those who are fighting for the natives with all their hearts and souls do not believe it, cannot believe it, cannot believe that this will be the end of all their efforts, that any such blot will foul the escutcheon of the United States. But if it be so, let at least the memorial of their names remain. When the inhabited wilderness has become an uninhabited wilderness, when the only people who will ever make their homes in it are exterminated, when the placer-gold is gone and the white men have gone also. when the last interior Alaskan town is like Diamond City and Glacier City and Bearpaw City and Roosevelt City; and Bettles and Rampart and Coldfoot; and Cleary City and Delta City and Vault City and a score of others; let at least the native names of these great mountains remain to show that there once dwelt in the land a simple, hardy race who braved successfully the rigors of its climate and the inhospitality of their environment and flourished, until the septic contact of a superior race put corruption into their blood. So this book shall end as it began.